Lucid Dreaming

The Ultimate Guide on How to Literally Live Your Dreams

(A Guide to Lucid Dreaming, Self-discovery, Consciousness, Dream Control & Dream Analysis)

John Adams

Published By **Chris David**

John Adams

All Rights Reserved

Lucid Dreaming: The Ultimate Guide on How to Literally Live Your Dreams (A Guide to Lucid Dreaming, Self-discovery, Consciousness, Dream Control & Dream Analysis)

ISBN 978-1-7771996-2-3

No part of this guidebook shall be reproduced in any form without permission in writing from the publisher except in the case of brief quotations embodied in critical articles or reviews.

Legal & Disclaimer

The information contained in this book is not designed to replace or take the place of any form of medicine or professional medical advice. The information in this book has been provided for educational & entertainment purposes only.

The information contained in this book has been compiled from sources deemed reliable, and it is accurate to the best of the Author's knowledge; however, the Author cannot guarantee its accuracy and validity and cannot be held liable for any errors or omissions. Changes are periodically made to this book. You must consult your doctor or get professional medical advice before using any of the suggested remedies, techniques, or information in this book.

Upon using the information contained in this book, you agree to hold harmless the Author from and against any damages, costs, and expenses, including any legal fees potentially resulting from the application of any of the information provided by this guide. This disclaimer applies to any damages or injury caused by the use and application, whether directly or indirectly, of any advice or information presented, whether for breach of contract, tort, negligence, personal injury, criminal intent, or under any other cause of action.

You agree to accept all risks of using the information presented inside this book. You need to consult a professional medical practitioner in order to ensure you are both able and healthy enough to participate in this program.

Table Of Contents

Chapter 1: Set Yourself For Lucid Dreaming Success 1

Chapter 2: Manifesting Dream Characters And Hacking Their Minds 9

Chapter 3: How To Create Dream Characters Without Difficulty................. 13

Chapter 4: Some Immoderate Subjects To Dream Approximately 21

Chapter 5: Dream Portals And Teleporting Into Different Worlds 29

Chapter 6: Get The Ones Dietary Supplements 42

Chapter 7: Manifesting Cash And Controlling Dream Characters................ 65

Chapter 8: Incense And Aromas............. 79

Chapter 9: What Are Lucid Dreams? 88

Chapter 10: States Of Consciousness ... 106

Chapter 11: What Is Awareness? 119

Chapter 12: A Route To Bed To Promote Good Sleep 135

Chapter 13: Long-Term Empowerment 151

Chapter 14: After Dreaming 165

Chapter 1: Set Yourself For Lucid Dreaming Success

Before we get into the main 'meat' of this eBook, we want to talk approximately a manner to set yourself up for lucid dreaming fulfillment. What I propose via this is you want to get geared up to have lucid desires.

To begin with, actually make certain you've have been given a jogging dream magazine next in your mattress, and also you're writing your desires down.

It's smooth to forget about this, and at the equal time as you realise the manner to lucid dream, to genuinely now not write any goals down but this is incorrect.

Even if you obviously don't forget loads of your dreams, you need to hold a dream magazine to look in which you went incorrect. You can write such things as what supplements you used, how they labored, how you felt the morning after and so on.

Also, things like experiments and lucid dreaming dreams need to be written in the magazine, in any other case you'll in no manner be capable of appearance again and see what you in all likelihood did, in that you're going proper and what you're doing incorrect. Make enjoy?

So earlier than we bypass any similarly, make certain you're preserving a dream journal, and that it's subsequent on your bed so you can without issue get right of access to it.

Basic weight loss plan and health setup for goals

I'll maintain this brief because it's simply the basics, but in case you want to optimise your mind for lucid desires you'll probably

want to be taking a multivitamin every morning, similarly to an Omega 3-6-nine tablet.

This offers your mind the whole lot it wants to well feature and restore itself and lots of others.

Another component you can check is becoming Vegan or specially plant based completely

(not essential, however I've discovered it allows in a big manner with mental and bodily health).

Wake up early: About five-6AM appears to be the fantastic time

 to evoke within the morning which however offers you sufficient sleep if you get to mattress on time, but furthermore helps you to experience most of the day and I discover my thoughts works outstanding waking up in the interim. Of course, take a look at for yourself and see what your frame responds well to!

Drink masses of water: Every day you have to drink as a minimum 7-eight glasses of filtered easy water

, as this is truely basics for any health plan! Your mind and body will revel in higher, believe me.

The GOLDEN rule for lucid dreaming manipulate

This is probably one of the maximum vital subjects you could discover about lucid desires. In a phrase, what you EXPECT to expose up, will take region.

Now, you can have already heard that but it's continuously well worth having a reminder. What I mean via this is that some component you located or take into account will take location, usually will because of the reality your unconscious mind desires to be proper.

In lucid goals the number one dream global (the physics, and the mechanism of the manner everything works) is controlled by using manner of your unconscious thoughts. You're best a bit little bit of a far larger photograph, even as you're lucid.

This manner it's such as you're taking walks round a modern-day global which you haven't any clue approximately, although it's certainly YOUR mind that's developing and controlling it all. It's a unusual concept, I understand however stay with me right here.

The blueprint that your subconscious mind creates and controls the lucid dream from isDrumroll please

Your unconscious ideals and expectancies approximately the world spherical you.

This technique that something you TRULY don't forget deep down approximately the arena, will generally take vicinity in a lucid dream. Now, of route there are exceptions due to the reality goals are very weird and don't commonly observe the 'rules' but in awesome, your ideals manipulate the dream.

For example, if you've been residing on this planet for brought than 5 years or so (even after three hundred and sixty 5 days in reality) for a FACT that in case you throw some factor up in the air, it comes down. (Gravity).

You apprehend this due to the fact you've seen it all the time and your entire lifestyles, no longer something one-of-a-kind has ever came about, so that belief has sunk into your unconscious in order that even in a dream, you assume subjects to fall on the identical time as you throw them up.

This is why maximum novices warfare to fly in lucid dreams, and why your lucid desires look like they're once in a while controlling you as an alternative the alternative way spherical.

Understand this idea and your lucid goals will in no way be the same, due to the reality you're opened up the essential issue of manipulate. If you TRULY persuade yourself that you're the only in control, and that some element you need to take place, you EXPECT to arise, you'll do extremely good topics.

Try it next time you're lucid.

Become lucid and then search around you and find out a automobile as an instance. Now, besides that at the same time as you snap your arms, the auto will shoot up into the air, with out you even touching it.

Then snap your hands. Nine times out of 10, if you sincerely believed it, the automobile will shoot up and you'll probably begin feeling all excited and walking throughout the dream shouting and so forth (and then probably wake your self up) but that's adequate!

So earlier than we pass on, definitely undergo that in thoughts. Think approximately the golden rule earlier than attempting to find to lucid dream, and the way your expectation will make the dream become real. It will help you at the same time as you get caught. There have been plenty of desires wherein I've been lucid, but been form of caught and out of vicinity manipulate..

But really remembering that golden rule helped me get again into lucidity and all over again on top of things. I belief 'Wait a minute, what do I EXPECT to reveal up now?' and then it does take region. It's almost like magic and it's a wonderful control approach for deciding what the dream does.

Advanced lucid dreaming adventures and testimonies

Here we're going to speak about topics you could do to make the lucid dreaming revel in greater immoderate and thrilling. This is stuff which you in all likelihood haven't tried but, however if there may be a few factor proper right here you've already tried, certainly bypass that factor.

You shouldn't genuinely be analyzing this thing if you may't already lucid dream, so if this have end up blanketed with extraordinary ebooks approximately lucid dreaming or in case you've presented this on it's private, learn how to lucid dream in advance than reading this next section.

From now on we'll count on that you may end up lucid, and people techniques or thoughts are supposed to be attempted on the equal time as you're lucid already.

Chapter 2: Manifesting Dream Characters And Hacking Their Minds

Dream characters are the ones people or various matters (they is probably extraterrestrial beings!) inside a dream that essentially upload to the dreaming experience. They're truely also a part of your subconscious mind.

They may be very beneficial and you may check masses about yourself through interacting with dream characters. Remember, because they're a part of YOU, they may be able to constitute incredible components of your thoughts and psyche.

You should, for example talk to the part of your thoughts that represents a fear you have got, and ask it WHY you have got that fear and so forth..

As the person developing your lucid dream, your dream characters may be made totally in your private liking. You can pick out to engage together together with your dream characters, or now not. Now on occasion, they will appear to behave or be created without your purpose. Most of the time definitely your dream characters are created robotically with the aid of way of your unconscious thoughts, so that you don't surely have any input. But you can learn how to manage it!

Your dream characters will often act reputedly in reality independant of you, the dreamer.

As you stroll via a lucid dream, it looks as if they're separate human beings, and function their very own free will. They can decide what to do and it's like you're interacting with actual real human beings.

In many approaches, dream characters add greater depth to your dream because they permit you a extra interactive lucid dreaming enjoy.

In a few techniques, dream characters may be likened to online game characters. In video video games, you because the participant get to pick the advent of YOUR particular avatar on the way to will will let you navigate via the online game. Likewise, there are numbers of various characters in the video game if you want to be interacting collectively along with your previously selected video game character.

This analogy the use of video game characters is just like dream characters. Just just like the video game individual that interacts with distinctive characters interior the sport, you because the lucid dreamer moreover have the possibility to interact with numerous dream characters as well.

So, why might you need to create dream characters? Well, dream characters serve pretty some features. They can be very beneficial!

You because the lucid dreamer can create the characters which can be maximum applicable to the context of your lucid dream. Some others enjoy that dream characters are a example of our psyches and deep private beliefs and reminiscences. Because of this, dream characters have a way of revealing masses about the subconscious 'goals and goals' of the lucid dreamer.

Try it subsequent time you're lucid, find out a dream individual (we'll communicate about the way to create them in a 2nd) after which ask them what they constitute!

It's a manner of 'hacking' their thoughts. Just through asking them questions like that, you get interior your very own head even more, and the solutions you'll pay interest can be virtually surprising. The exceptional manner of doing that is definitely to turn out to be lucid the use of a few issue method you need, discover a dream individual after which ask them 'what are you?'.

Chapter 3: How To Create Dream Characters Without Difficulty

Here are some strategies that you could have higher fulfillment at growing dream characters:

It is vital to have a look at that earlier than you even begin developing dream characters, it's vital to have a business enterprise hold close of lucid dreaming. You have with a view to frequently take manage of your desires before you even begin the way of seeking to create dream characters internal a dream environment.

1: Shapeshifting

Shape-shifting is a very exciting way to create the dream characters which you desire. Essentially you'll be the usage of any item within your dream u . S Shape-moving in reality includes WILLING that specific inanimate item into the dream person that you desire.

This can also take a few exercise, however when you've achieved shapeshifting an item right right into a dream character you may discover that this technique is one of the coolest ways to create dream characters in a lucid dreaming environment. Start through using certainly searching at a random object like a vehicle, and then inform your self 'as quickly as I click on on my arms, the car will grow to be a dream person'.

Trust me, if you remember it strongly sufficient it's going to manifest, and actually you don't even need lots perception to get it to show up. Usually I may want to make this occur clearly with the aid of imagining the change or visualising the auto converting into the dream individual. You would possibly possibly want to exercising this one a bit and it could now not paintings first time.

I find out the extra strongly you may visualise the alternate, the faster it takes place. It's moreover beneficial to stabilise the lucid dream in advance than trying this, because of the reality the shape transferring can have a propensity to shake the fabric of the dream a bit!

2: Using Dream Doors

Imagine starting a door for your lucid dream and accomplishing within the darkish depths of the door and in fact pulling out the dream individual which you desire. Seems pretty a ways-fetched, huh? Well, really it's not.

Dream doorways or portals

are a super way door to create a dream individual, you in reality need to have the expectancy that your dream man or woman is in the back of that door. It's all based totally at the power of your expectations and intentions.

Start by way of way of way of becoming lucid, and then discover a door or portal. A portal must absolutely simply be a window certainly, or a hollow or a few issue that you could ENTER. Imagine pulling a dream individual outOr believe a dream individual sincerely strolling out of the door or window.

Now stare closely on the portal or door. Tell your self 'in a second, a dream individual will walk thru that door' after which clearly stare at the door. But don't stare as if you're SEEING if it's going to work.

Stare at it as you may at the same time as looking beforehand to a friend to expose up. As if you KNOW it's going to show up and they're without a doubt next door, and also you're just ready to appearance them come next door. Imagine the sensation you have interior you while you've genuinely called your friend you're meeting up with, and that they said they could see you and that they're virtually down the street. That feeling even as you test the distance looking in advance to to see them rapid.

That's the feeling you need to have at the same time as watching the dream portal or door. If you may get that feeling, you'll make this art work I promise.

three: Ask the lucid dream itself

If you need a particular form of dream person in a dream, why not truely sincerely ask for it? Yes, you could ask your dream to provide you with the dream character of your desire.

Remember, with lucid dreaming you're the one on top of factors most of the time. Your lucid dreaming revel in is completely up to you for the maximum element. The dreamscape feeds off of your needs and dreams.

Therefore, it is viable that allows you to surely ASK your dream to create the characters which you want and apprehend that the characters will appear.

With this method, you because the lucid dreamer need to have a deep understanding and expertise that the dream responds to you in order for this technique to paintings.

Dream commands

moreover may be used to do almost some thing in a lucid dream.

I've managed to enjoy a few extremely good matters honestly with the beneficial resource of asking the dream to show me those matters. In fact the dream itself can absolutely surprise you, and in case you ask the dream to show you a few thing you're now not looking ahead to? Oh manThat's a huge wonder right there. The dream is of path created with the useful resource of your unconscious mind, and maximum people have NO IDEA how powerful and complicated that part of your mind honestly is.

By asking the unconscious to surprise you, you're taken on a rollercoaster of revel in. It's like tumbling down the rabbit hollow! So the next time you're in a lucid dream, attempt asking the dream to surprise you, or create a dream character for you and plenty of others.

4: Create an Image with Your Mind's Eye

Finally, using your mind's eye at the same time as in a lucid dreaming kingdom it's definitely a awesome manner to create dream characters without problems.

Whether you pick to color an picture of the dream character in order to introduce it to a dream surroundings or possibly the usage of a college method of piecing together someone is more your fashion, the entire factor is that the vision of your dream character starts offevolved with you.

You truely need to apprehend in particular what you need your dream person to appearance and be like so as if you want to create that during your dream global reality.

Ultimately, developing dream characters isn't as tough as it is able to appear. Once you have got were given a agency keep near of lucid dreaming and recognize the importance of expectation and goal within the lucid dreaming manner, you'll be in your way to developing dream characters without problem.

Try this subsequent time you're lucid: Create a dream person based totally totally on YOU. Or genuinely find out a replica of your self in the lucid dream and communicate to yourself. You'll be surprised at how many complex and profound solutions he/she has!

Chapter 4: Some Immoderate Subjects To Dream Approximately

Here are some crazy subjects you can try and lucid dream approximately. These topics are going to be intense with the resource of the manner, so ensure you're prepared.

1: Go to a social occasion with bugs

The animal and bug worlds are left often undisturbed all of the time! They in all likelihood have social gatherings too! Now earlier than the guys in white coats come to take me away to the satisfied farm, I suggest in desires. In goals, you may engage with ideas, animals, bugs and some thing else.

Find a meeting of wasps, and sit down down down in on their tea party! It will be very just like Alice in Wonderland and you'll find out your self curious about their stories, jokes and mannerisms. When I inform human beings such things as this in my movies or thru electronic mail it may be funny. People have in all likelihood by no means tried things like this and it could be highly specific from what they've attempted before in dreams.

It's a awesome manner of experiencing new things. Also via manner of trying topics which might be thus far from what yo've USUALLY achieved in dreams in advance than, you're growing. Your lucid dreaming skills have become stronger and also you're becoming greater of a lucid hold close.

2: Enter a painting

Paintings and drawings are complete worlds equipped to be entered in lucid desires. You can truly walk into them just like you'd walk proper right into a door. For those of you who've seen or observe Narnia stories, (the voyage of the Dawntreader)it's like after they input the portray of the boat and are transported to the scene, with the water flooding into the room and right away pulling them into the scene.

Often you may enter the portray or photo in a lucid dream simply with the useful resource of strolling as plenty as it and urgent yourself closer to it. Sometimes however, in case you're no longer absolutely looking ahead to that lets in you to do that, you'll turn out to be definitely half caught within the wall and that can be annoying.

three: Become superman and start a fight

If you've seen Superman then you definately definately'll recognise how amazing it need to appearance to be invincible and able to fly at supersonic speeds. Next lucid dream, make yourself into the superhero and fly spherical, preventing simply all people who desires to save you you!

Superman or one-of-a-kind superheros are first-rate fun to turn out to be and mess around with. I like flying or transferring objects with my thoughts the use of telekinesis!

four: Lift a skyscraper with one hand

Another superhuman potential. Lifting definitely heavy topics with simply one hand is a commonplace use of lucidity. To workout this, in waking life you're going to workout the superpower by using manner of the usage of PHYSICALLY setting your hand on heavy gadgets, and imagining what it might sense like if you were capable of increase them effortlessly.

Practice just setting your hand on a automobile (at some stage within the day) and questioning 'I can elevate this with out trouble if I really attempt). This primes your subconscious mind and ideals so that you can do the identical in lucid dreams. Tell your self that the heavy objects are truly weightless, and you'll be capable of boom them!

five: Build a metropolis together together with your thoughts

Just like if you have been a infant an you performed with Lego to assemble small cities (or now not, I do not recognise) you can assemble a metropolis collectively at the side of your mind in a dream. Rise above the gap thru flying up, after which stretch out your hand. Imagine the metropolis is constructing itself but you are on top of things of what gets built.

You can assemble whole towns in seconds, and you may fast forward time to appearance how the humans in them change and behave over the years. See what wonderful houses they assemble and what happens to their lives!

6: Grow a forest collectively along with your hands

You can create life in precisely the identical way you'd wreck it in lucid dreams. One of the most fun sports is to develop such things as timber or forests together collectively together with your thoughts powers. Look on the floor in the the front of you and recollect the energy and life pressure coming for the floor, via your frame, via your hand and into the region you're searching at.

Imagine the life force building a lifestyles shape like a tree, and then pace it up. You can increase a whole forest in seconds, and you could even move your hand the possibility way to opposite the approach and notice the timber develop once more into the ground.

7: Visit the 3 hundred and sixty five days 19013894

Most folks have mind approximately what the future can be like based films and testimonies, however how accurate are they? The truth is the destiny probable appears NOTHING like we're imagining it, and might be finished unique to some thing we understand these days.

Ask the dream to expose you 2308420325 years into the destiny and you'll be surprised at what you offer you with. I've accomplished this numerous instances and it's one among a kind every time.

One time there was certainly not something, in fact blackness (I bet in that fact, we wiped ourselves out with bombs?). Other instances, it's been a cute array of lights and strength, similar to a firework show. I wager this is a fact where we've managed to expose ourselves into herbal electricity and don't need human our our bodies any more. See what your mind comes up with!

8: Ask the dream to take you to the start of existence

What become the arena like on the very start of lifestyles? Was it a large bang, or did we evolve? Was there a writer? All excellent questions which we without a doubt in no way without a doubt understand for effective. We can theorise, and some theories can seem much more likely than others however we absolutely don't recognize for 100%. In your next lucid dream ask your thoughts to take you to the begin of lifestyles.

When you attempt these objects, make sure you write them down in a dream journal. This will help you be conscious what different things felt like. You'll moreover need to put in writing down ANY dream symptoms or subjects that took place in extra than 2 goals. This might be essential in some time.

In truth I'd truly endorse definitely trying each of these gadgets in separate goals so that you can supply your thoughts the first-rate threat of getting a very specific revel in on every occasion. You don't need those to intrude with eachother.

Chapter 5: Dream Portals And Teleporting Into Different Worlds

A lucid portal is some issue inside the dream that could shipping you from one location to every exclusive. (Or one time to every specific). It's a few element you can step thru or into, like a replicate or a doorway..

They additionally may be in different sorts like a slide, tube, trapdoor, hole within the ground, misty air of thriller and so on. They can are available in many forms, but the key is that they typically take you somewhere very quickly.

They may be located everywhere, however commonly your mind will region them into places that usually have entrances or doors you can stroll thru.

This is truely the proper opportunity to test your lucid portals, find out a lengthy street with many houses on every problem, and begin organising all the doors to look what's the other side.

You'll quick discover that it's no longer sincerely someone's residence, it may be a few different worldwide. This is due to the fact your mind creates matters thru doorways in dreams that don't always 'blend' with the relaxation of the dream.

How to discover and enter a lucid portal

Here's how you can locate dream portals with out trouble, and use them to journey via a dream international. Remember that the KEY with dream portals is expectation and perception. If you in truth recall a portal will take you somewhere, it will!

1: Decide in that you need to move

The first step to the use of dream portals is thinking about in which it's miles you want to go. Try and provide you with a clean photo of the region to your mind, earlier than you even try to find out a portal. Think about whether or not you've been there in advance than, or what is going to be there while you arrive.

The more emotional you could get your reaction, the higher. If you can get clearly scared and concerned, OR truely excited and satisfied approximately the issue, you'll get there less difficult. Emotions and expectancies are the two maximum vital subjects in lucid desires.

2: Find a herbal doorway or starting

In goals, there are nearly continuously matters that reflect waking existence. These subjects can be effortlessly used as portals, because dream physics are NOT like real international physics.

You must open a tiny door to a mobile telephone booth and discover some different planet at the opportunity thing of the door. Here are some examples of herbal openings or doorways:

Door or door frames

Trapdoors inside the floor

Shower curtains or drapes in houses

Any window in any building

You need to attract a trapdoor with chalk at the ground

3: Expect to journey through it

Look at the entrance you've placed or created, and inform your self: 'I'm going to adventure via this portal and arrive on the alternative side in my place (some thing place you want to go to). Notice that you don't HAVE to decide in which to go to! You can sincerely permit the dream wonder you!

4: Explore the vacation spot

When you enter the place on the alternative side, genuinely discover it really and don't panic! It may not be exactly what you predicted but it need to be quite close! If you virtually permit the dream surprise you, then find out it! You might be anywhere!

Focus on what you WANT to be there

Sometimes certainly walking via you'll locate random topics, and this will be appropriate in case you're sincerely in search of to find out and discover the dream however in case you've were given particular lucid desires and you're seeking to get a few factor done on this lucid time, it's important to attention as you enter the lucid portal.

Making the dreams extra strong

Lots of humans discover that they clearly wake up too quickly from their Lucid research and discover it very tough to get lower back to their previous mental united states of america.

This goes to assist those humans thru prolonging their dreams. When you find out yourself fading out of a Lucid Dream, spin spherical at once.

Stand instant and virtually spin spherical. Not too speedy, but no longer too gradual every. Just spin at the charge you'll in real lifestyles and while doing so, 'will' yourself to live in the dream. Tell your self that you'll live inside the dream, and more frequently than now not you certainly will.

Spinning spherical in a lucid dream

This works by the use of forcing you to reputation on some thing bodily. Many of the dream stabilisation strategies art work on this manner or even virtually that specialize in some aspect unique like searching at the detail for your hands at the same time as in a dream can extend it. It focuses your mind and relaxes you forcing you to live underneath for longer.

Doing such things as dropping to the ground in a dream in hopes to stabilise and reputation you can produce other results however. It's been said that 'falling down' clearly makes you wake up – or THINK you've woken up; you have got were given a fake awakening. We'll preserve on with the spinning approach for now. Here's the way to do it:

Step 1: Focus your self and Set your intentions

The first level with that is to set your intentions which can be that you need to become a touch more focused within the dream and in the long run save you yourself from waking up right now.

You don't want to evoke the second while you've become Lucid so that you can spin spherical to make it very last longer. That's the purpose right here so make certain to simply cement this on your mind earlier than you sincerely spin.

The motive you want to cement the aim to your thoughts first is that humans often find out that in the occasion that they genuinely spin with none intention they end up in a random location; they've changed dream scenes and don't understand wherein they'll be of what just occurred.

It can have the opposite impact in case you spin to attempt to loosen up and stabilise and then on the identical time as you forestall spinning you're balanced at the top of a skyscrape searching down!

Step 2: Spin!

This is in that you simply spin round, whilst searching on the floor. Try not to shut your eyes in the dream as this almost normally ends in waking up or to 'faux awakenings' which aren't first-rate. Spin spherical at a mild velocity searching on the ground.

Step 3: Reality take a look at/stay calm

Once you've stopped spinning you'll discover which you're greater targeted and the dream appears to have become clearer.

If now not, try each one of a kind stabilisation method like searching at your fingers or rubbing them collectively and so forth, however it should be hundreds clearer now. You also can want to reality check proper now or loosen up and pick out a mild stroll within the dream.

Some fact tests you may attempt at this degree are:

Pushing your finger through your palm

Reading text to see if you can apprehend it

Checking your watch to look if the time adjustments

Looking spherical to look if some thing seems great to you

Using nutritional dietary dietary supplements to stabilise the dream

If you're a long time lucid dreamer, the opportunities are you are looking for something MORE. You know you could do greater with lucid dreaming, you surely don't comprehend how.

Well, nutritional supplements is probably the solution. With nutritional supplements, you can take your lucid dreaming to each distinct degree. They're really useful! We are fortunate nowadays due to the reality there are DOZENS of lucid dreaming capsules on the market. I desire there were this many as quickly as I first started out out.

Here's a precis of the maximum not unusual lucid dreaming drugs and the way they paintings:

There are many specific drugs and supplements available, and they all have an impact on desires in slightly considered one of a type strategies. We'll provide an cause of a number of the easy ones, and the maximum not unusual. There are sincerely loads of them to be had, and it's very essential to understand as an awful lot as you can about them in advance than you operate them, if dubious, don't use it.

1: Calea Zacatechichi (The dream herb)

This is a small Mexican plant which even as the leaves are ingested produces powerful dream consequences. It increase the clarity of the dream, makes it experience 'extra real' and makes the dream final longer.

It's also recognize because the Dream Herb, Leaf of god, Bitter Grass and so forth. It's stated to taste disgusting at the same time as below the influence of alcohol in a tea, and that after it's smoked, the smoke may be very dry and tough.

It's been stated that the great manner to take Calea Zacatechichi for dreaming is to overwhelm the leaves and smoke them via a water filtered bong, ideally with ice to take a seat again the smoke, making it smoother to take in.

2: Vitamin B6

This is a nutrients supplement that's said as a manner to make your dreams greater vivid, and particularly beautify dream consider. It's now and again recognize due to the fact the 'dream tablet' because it's very powerful at enhancing your dream undergo in mind, and helping you to bear in mind what you dream about.

three: Galantamine

Galantamine is probably one of the more harsh dietary dietary dietary supplements you may attempt. Still clearly really worth a skip however undergo in thoughts it could be a piece difficult to your body and people report feeling a chunk ill occasionally in this one.

four: LucidEsc by Vividream

Lucidesc

is An effective, natural lucid complement designed that will help you grow to be lucid while you sleep. This is genuinely a super one for all and sundry as it's no longer harsh on your body and it really works thoroughly!

five: Melatonin

Melatonin has the strength to have an effect on lucid goals in a large manner. This is more of a hormone however I felt it equipped in proper here. It's the hormone that makes you feel worn-out at night time and can be used to have deeper and extra vibrant dreams while taken on the right dosage.

6: Mugwort

Mugwort is clearly greater of a herb

however I'd locate it irresistible to be on this net web page. It may be used to make a 'dream pillow and high-quality lucid aids. Very cheap, now not as effective as one-of-a-type dietary supplements but.

7: Choline bitartrate

Choline can provide you with higher dream reminiscence

however it has unique benefits as properly. It is greater of a memory boosting complement that has strong hyperlinks to lucid dreaming.

8: DreamLeaf (The purple and blue drugs)

These fantastically designed tablets

are modelled on the colours from The Matrix. Containing active and effective lucid dreaming components, they're a great choice for newbie lucid dreamers!

Chapter 6: Get The Ones Dietary Supplements

The exceptional region to get these supplements is a put up I wrote evaluating they all and reviewing the amazing lucid dreaming dietary supplements. It's an in depth put up however there are clean links to each supplement said right here and hundreds extra.

There are ALSO plenty of reductions I've managed to get you men so in case you want to investigate extra approximately those nutritional dietary supplements and get reductions, take a look at out the 'ebook bonus' section at the quit of this e-book, which has a totally particular listing of discounts and facts for you.

Stopping/slowing down time in dreams

Do you want so that you can control your belief of time in a lucid dream? Turns out you can actually stop time on the equal time as you're lucid, and extend the lucid dream.

Time, in reality, is to three diploma, subjective. What may additionally appear to be a long time to at least one individual can seem like a brief time for any other. It is based upon at the people belief of strategies slowly or brief time is passing, and therefore in a dream, we want as a way to exchange our belief and consequently save you time in a dream!

So to try this, as with maximum of the lucid suggestions demonstrated in this net website on line, you will of path want to be strong with your reality tests, and the identical antique matters you will do to come to be lucid and live alert in the dream. I do not want to remind you approximately all of that stuff.

Shout out 'Stop time!' to the dream itself

Believe it or not, when you're lucid,

shouting out instructions

like 'forestall time' in reality art work a number of the time. Because you are almost speaking in your unconscious mind you're capable of be quite precise approximately what you need to appear.

By genuinely shouting out to the dream worldwide, you could get maximum of your instructions replied, but there are pretty a few times in which this may no longer art work. If you are now not lucid enough and also you do now not believe some thing will trade, it might not, It's plenty like in The Matrix wherein Neo is analyzing to 'make the leap'.

Any small doubts approximately his capability and he is going to fall, and it's far this that applies proper here. If you shout out a command like 'time will stop' to the dream, and you are genuinely form of ready to look if it'll occur, it probably won't. You need to shout it out as if you're wonderful it'll happen.

Almost such as you recognize past a doubt that factor will save you. If this is proving hard, then you in reality would possibly need to try some one of a kind mind earlier than you can without a doubt make time come to an entire halt. Dreams are a flowery difficulty to realize, but it's miles all viable.

You'll furthermore discover that the greater you take a look at and the most you try to range the abilities you check, the quicker you will improvement.

Slowing down time in a dream

So in case you're struggling with preventing time completely, you can discover it an awful lot much less complicated to really gradual it down at the beginning. Slowing it down will make it look like every body else round you is transferring slower manifestly, but you will be moving at regular pace.

There's continuously a bit little bit of confusion with slowing down time or preventing time, due to the fact one among subjects are taking place to you. (This has been shown in films collectively with X-Men, Days of future past).

You make time come to a halt, but you could waft round at regular velocity

OR

You tempo YOURSELF as much as such an quantity that the whole lot else seems to be frozen but in truth you are simply transferring really, simply fast

In the dream, it would now not certainly rely which of those display up, because with each of them, you'll subjectively revel in time slowing down or preventing. This brings me to the approach you may be using the gradual down time in a dream.

It's all approximately your feelings and your mind. You're going to 'anticipate' simply rapid'. Instead of focusing on the sector round you and trying to make that every one slow down, you'll speed your self up and this can in flip gradual the rest of the world down.

Some affirmations or mind you could need to start having at this diploma are:

'I'm transferring so fast that the whole lot spherical me is hardly ever moving in any respect'

'I can pass at lightning pace at some stage in the dream international'

Saying those both to your head to your self or out loud within the dream will begin slowing time in the dream. While announcing or questioning those statements, try going for walks or moving round as nicely, look around you for strategies to check how rapid you're going.

Maybe find out a dream person, run round him and tap him on the another time, then zoom spherical to the the front before he can turn.

At this point, he have to be transferring absolutely slowly. (Or you're moving right away) and it's going to supply the experience of time having bogged down.

Your belief of time is based definitely throughout the belongings you do and the locations you skip in a dream, so as you are able to tour speedy - Almost right now - Time can appear to be it is going thru faster and you are spending longer inside the dream.

Interesting lucid dreaming experiments

When you get into advanced lucid dreaming, one of the BEST subjects you can do is to set your self goals and demanding situations to do. It's all very well just flying spherical, however you may need to push your self to do greater in the end.

What you can do, is to set your self those goals earlier than you go to bed after which attempt to collect them for your lucid goals. Here are some very exciting goals or experiments you may strive in a lucid dream:

1: Telling your dream characters they're in a dream

What do you discovered ought to arise while you inform your dream character they're in a Lucid Dream?

Would they emerge as Lucid with you?

Well, it honestly relies upon on how conscious and in control you're, but in case you're on top of things and you've grounded yourself properly inside the dream the dream characters can also become Lucid with you.

It's a way of advancing via the awesome 'layers of a lucid dream' and going deeper into your mind. I'm no longer going to inform you what in reality takes area with this one as I assume it's extra interesting to try it with out looking in advance to some problem precise to appear.

I'll warn you presently despite the fact that, it's going to be excessive and you could WANT to make certain you're able to write your dreams down in the morning. This isn't always a dream you'll need to overlook. Having said that I don't think you'll be ABLE to miss this one very without troubles.

2: Talking to your nightmares

Ever been so afraid of some thing that you genuinely can't stand even considering it, not to mention speakme about it? For me, it turned into dogs, and wasps.

I emerge as fearful of them, however then in a Lucid Dream, I located a canine and in reality asked it, 'Why am I frightened of you' and it replied something along the strains of 'you've got been chased thru one as a young toddler and you haven't without a doubt steady the worry that got here because of that. You also have minor accept as true with issues, so you don't consider that puppies received't chase once you over again'.

Pretty eye beginning for me, and the equal form of problem passed off once I asked a wasp the same problem in a dream. Turns out I have been given stung when I changed into four and will have died.

I attempted to select up a wasp, due to the reality I concept it regarded pretty and favored to domestic dog it, it then stung me and (due to the reality the wasp defined in the dream). I consequently advanced moderate keep in mind problems and a deep seated fear of wasps. It took YEARS for me to repair that hassle and Lucid Dreaming is right away accountable for assisting me with that.

I discover that kind of hassle captivating. The fact that you may straight away interact with or perhaps CHANGE fears and phobias definitely with the aid of speakme to them without delay in a dream. It opens up the door to all kinds of other questions, and you start questioning honestly how lots you could change about your mind with lucid goals.

three: Look proper right into a reflect!

When you test a mirror in real lifestyles, you word that it's an real instance of you, (obviously). The prison guidelines physics are at play and so that you MUST see exactly the way you look.

In a dream of direction physics and each different laws are non-existent, therefore looking right into a replicate in a dream can display you masses approximately your self and the manner you're feeling about yourself.

It's

a touch bit like your residual self image

, which I've spoken about earlier than. A blueprint of what you consider you studied you ought to look like stored to your mind. Finding a reflect allows you to look in top notch element precisely the form of character you consider you studied you're.

The frightening aspect however, is that from time to time we can see matters which we usually overlook about in a dream reflect. We can appreciably exaggerate physical flaws and imperfections and it may appearance absolutely scary.

four: Speak to a psychiatrist/counsellor

Your subconscious thoughts is a captivating issue to speak to. Really, simply search a town for a counsellor in a dream and sit down and talk to them. It will display topics to you that you in no manner ought to have realised earlier than.

You also can type of ask the dream questions, and it normally will respond with some detail interesting. You don't really need to recognize particularly the manner to find out a dream manual or counsellor, due to the reality your mind will work it out. Just stroll spherical saying out loud 'in which's my dream counsellor' and also you'll locate it.

5: Travel in time and meet your self within the future

This is a in fact proper check to discover what you surely hold in mind your desires and aspirations.

Do you TRULY agree with you'll attain your desires and goals? If so, you'll meet a elegant, a fulfillment and outstanding version of yourself within the destiny and also you'll wake up feeling induced and stimulated.

If you don't don't forget in yourself, it's going to come out within the dream. You can't trick your subconscious thoughts, (resultseasily) and often it's miles going to show you a cruel illustration of your beliefs and mind within the path of your self.

Convincing a dream individual they're in a dream

What takes place even as you persuade a dream man or woman that they're in a lucid dream?

Convince them that their global isn't real…

You have to pretty effects display it to them, so what might they do when they realize it? Telling a dream man or woman that they're no longer actual and it's all a dream is an high-quality take a look at to try on your subsequent lucid dreamHere's what occurred as quickly as I attempted it:

Convincing a dream individual to come to be lucid with me

This is the tale of a dream I currently had as soon as I satisfied a person his worldwide wasn't real. I started the dream off like a few other, by way of manner of doing a truth check on the equal time as within the middle of a few random movement, I expect it changed into sitting at a table with my friend and as were have been discussing the weather I checked out my palms.

This precipitated a truth take a look at, I in reality have grow to be right now conscious that this wasn't actual, and so I appeared up at my buddy, and requested him 'Where did we just come from?'.

'What do you suggest? We surely came from cityWe spent the day shopping, don't forget?'

No, we didn't. I idea about a way to offer an reason behind this to him..

'We're in a dream' – 'This isn't real'.

He appeared confused, almost a chunk scared, now not scared that it's a dream, however scared that I'm loopy or performing bizarre. Just to be sure of myself, I did any other fact test, and my finger handed thru my palm.

'This simply is a dream, and I can show it', I said this not pretty know-how what to expect.

As I used telekinesis to move a plate throughout the table, he ultimately agreed that this turned into in truth a dream. This is at the same time as it have been given weird for me.

He snapped into a very terrific man or woman. As if his body had simply been possessed, and checked out me right now in my eyes. 'What are you doing in proper hereIn this a part of your thoughts?'. He shouted this at me.

I didn't recognize what to say.

Who have become this dream person now representing?

What a part of my mind became he?

I had no concept, and started out to expect I have become a bit out of my depth, but I stored on. I explained that I realise it's a dream and preferred to see what may arise if

I cautioned him. We then went for a walk outdoor, and what become the door emerge as a protracted hall.

This stretched on for what seemed like miles, and as we walked I persevered to ask him what he representedHe wouldn't inform me, however insisted that I become 'On the proper course'. Although I modified into aware and really on top of things, when I attempted changing subjects he stopped me

I attempted transferring scenes and just teleporting away, however he had a few form of effective power that held me in region.

I modified into now not capable of bypass.

It definitely have been given a touch frightening, and at one factor I attempted to wake up, but I couldn't. It modified into like being trapped indoors my private thoughtsI knew thoroughly that my body turn out to be laying there, asleep, and but in spite of the reality that I turn out to be lucid I couldn't break a long way from this dream person who had turn out to be effective and aware.

He assured me that it's good enough, and there's no longer anything to worry about, so we stored walking. Through every of the doorways, he confirmed me some aspect I had positioned out from the past. A lesson decided from various situations or activities, and he stated that it become 'the start of a unique adventure'. 'Lucid Dreaming is simplest the begin' he said.

As we walked, we endured to talk, and he gave me some recommendation and effective insights into my thoughts and the manner it worked which I can't share proper here as it's an extended way too non-public, but what I can say is that

It's as despite the fact that your mind is ready unfastened. I don't apprehend what's going on scientifically right here, but all I understand is that I became lucid inner my thoughts, and I had glad some different part of my mind that 'it' too ought to end up lucid.

The gateway to 'The larger photo'

This might be the maximum profound difficulty I've accomplished in lucid dreaming to date. It's nearly lifestyles changing, but I obtained't preserve on lest you positioned I'm exaggerating or making it up.

Try it for your self, make certain you're truely aware and strong in the dream yourself, and then convince someone they're in a dream.

See what a part of your thoughts it turns into and what will take place. Remember, even though at times it could appear horrifying, or maybe a touch bit unstable while you suppose you 'can't escape the dream', you may in no way get stuck in a lucid dream, don't fear about that. Just loosen up, and experience the experience.

It's opened my mind in a manner that's in no way occurred earlier than, all because I instructed a dream man or woman he's in a dream. I strongly propose that everybody who's even a hint bit into lucid dreaming need to do that, as it's one-of-a-kind for all people.

Dissolving the dream u. S. (INTENSE)

I've been controlling my desires for a few years now but this turned into a few aspect simply new to me. I controlled to 'cross past' the dream nation and in fact dissolve the dream kingdom into herbal consciousness.

This is greater of a touch story than an educational, due to the fact this is some factor that you can form of bet the manner to do your self even as you're lucid. It's self explanatory, except right here's the tale:

Before I start explaining this awesome dream I had, I need to make it smooth that this is without a doubt my revel in and my description of what I skilled.

I'm now not making unique claims that I've finished enlightenment, reached 'herbal focus' or some component like that. I'm genuinely going to describe the dream that I had, make of it what you'll.

It began as a everyday dream..

It began out out as I turn out to be having a normal dream. I were given into bed and begin to lighten up. I wasn't looking to result in lucidity, I changed into without a doubt surely worn-out and favored to sleep. Some nights are like that, you don't need to TRY and lucid dream, you honestly type of 'permit skip' to the bed and simply go with the flow into dream global.

I laid there for approximately five minutes after which began to lose reputation. I wasn't trying to live aware, so this wasn't a problem.

A few hours later

(I'm guessing, because of the fact I awoke rapidly after the whole dream at approximately 9AM)

I started to have a sequence of lengthy, complicated desires.

These goals had been barely private, so I acquired't percent all the statistics, however they had been a aggregate of reliving work days, a few conversations with various ex-partners and an journey to try to strength over a few water.

Random stuff, I recognise. After those dreams, I find myself walking down a road in a crowded city. I capture the reflection of myself in one of the home home windows and word that some issue is a bit amazing about my blouse.

It's a small element, however it makes me consider how I were given to in which I modified into. 'How did I get to this road? I don't bear in mind taking walks here' I asked myself.

So then I did a reality test. I tried to push my finger via my palm, (that is my fine fact test) and proper away have become lucid.

Now, at this difficulty, I should element out that it wasn't most effective a regular lucid dream. The second I have become Lucid, I knew a few factor have come to be one-of-a-type. It felt sharper, greater brilliant and really actual. It felt nearly like I couldn't awaken despite the fact that I preferred to.

In most lucid goals, all of the on the identical time as you're lucid you have were given got an low-priced grasp at the scenario and if you want to rouse, you typically can. That changed into not the case on this dream. I regarded around and started manipulating topics. The maximum fun element for me recently in lucid desires is to move gadgets with my thoughts the use of telekinesis.

I started out out out lifting small devices and moving them spherical. I had no 'cause' at this element, I became truely gambling being lucid and loose. I even have turn out to be taking part in just being in my very own little international and playing spherical. Some goals are like that, you just want to be playful and enjoy your self.

So the dream went on, and I persisted exploring. The longer I stayed within the dream, the clearer it have come to be. I started out out out to get used to the sensation of it and it felt like I'd been there for hours, perhaps even days. As I explored an increasing number of I fell in love with the feeling.

It have become one-of-a-kind to my different lucid desires. This one really felt 'right'. I felt like I have become exactly in which I needed to be at that issue, regardless of the truth that I didn't complete understand what become happening.

Chapter 7: Manifesting Cash And Controlling Dream Characters

I attempted various subjects out from this factor on. Firstly, I had been trying to make more money at art work the beyond few weeks, so this went via to my dreaming mind.

I commenced manifesting cash in my hand. I imagined a stack of £50 notes and that they seemed in my hand. I threw them away and began out to growth wooden from the ground.

I'd test in which I favored to boom the tree, keep my hand out and push a load of power through the air into the floor. The tree without delay commenced out to boom and inner some seconds it changed into towering above me. Pretty cool, but I favored to do greater.

I mess around a few more and begin to govern the alternative dream characters. I determine wherein they're going to stroll and what they're going to say. This is amusing for a while. After a few minutes of this, I keep my arms out to my facets and look up at the sky. I experience so effective, and however so free at the same time.

It's all very easy. I surprise at this point how I've now not woken up however, as I've completed pretty a few interesting things and typically I can tell when I'm about to evoke fro the lucid nation. Not this time. This time the dream simply stayed positioned. I couldn't shake it if I wanted to.

I appeared lower again at the sky and started out out to float gently on my back. At this degree I felt absolutely comfortable. I felt like a king looking down on his nation from his fortress.

Trying to discover my dream guide

When I got here again to a status role, I modified into somewhere new. I had a few human beings walking with the useful useful resource of me and I decided to try to discover my dream guide.

The SECOND I had this concept, the scene regarded to at once trade. I discovered the dream characters test my in every other way, as though that that that they had woken up or they knew some thing I didn't.

I search around and some human beings appearance lower lower back at me. I don't say a few factor, but I surely have the aim of locating my dream guide. Someone to assist me via the dream and supply me some thoughts as to what to do next. After all, this seemed like a stable dream and I didn't need to waste it any extra by using using throwing vehicles spherical.

After a few seconds, a peculiar guy seems to certainly appear at my facet and appears at me as though he's checking that I'm alive. It's like he's looking to schooling consultation if I'm actually right right here or not, and it's very off-setting and unusual for me.

A communication with my lucid dream guide

I ask him if he's a dream guide and he says 'Yes of path I am'. He takes me to a futuristic searching town and we stroll to a area in which there's a sort of essential 'rectangular' or clearing. Skyscrapers rise up into the clouds all spherical us and the city is alive with noises and loads of movement.

We then have a communication as human beings (aliens, robots and businessmen) stroll round us going about their day..

Me – Where are we?

Dream Guide – 'This is the 'entrance'. This is in which humans input the dream and connect with do business company offers of all sorts'

Me – What do you imply? What form of industrial corporation offers?

Dream Guide – (I can't bear in mind an appropriate way he stated this however I'll attempt) 'Well, humans from anywhere within the universe come together right here among specific places, to do organisation gives. Some of them have transcended time and they get collectively right here to artwork on 'timelines' and 'restoration matters' in history'

Me – 'Wow, that's awesome. Why did you supply me here?'

Dream Guide – (Again at this element he appears into my eyes and looks to be 'checking' that I'm in truth reputation there and not truly an phantasm) 'I count on you're ready to look this. I've been searching you boom, decrease again for your lucid goals, and I assume you're organized for the subsequent step'

Me – What do you mean, 'another time in my desires'?

Dream Guide – 'If you haven't located, you're not the handiest dreamer on this vicinity'

Me – 'What are you speaking about, that is my dream! I'm on top of things right here I'm in fact letting you display me some detail'

Dream Guide (At this point he seems at me the way a determine would look at a infant getting to know to stroll, a type of loving, statistics appearance) – 'We had been in your dream, however I've added you proper right here to take a look at some component'

At this degree, multiple different human beings input our conversation. We're honestly popularity there in the middle of this place on this futuristic town, and a man wearing a in shape with each one of a kind man sporting a leather-based-primarily based trench coat rise up to us.

They tell me that they're dreamers too, and that I should be cautious with stating that it's my dream and I'm on top of factors in this area. It can be volatile, they tell me. Now, I haven't organized for a deep dream like this.

The preceding night time I have been consuming a bit bit, and I hadn't finished any shape of meditation or prep artwork for this, so my dreaming thoughts is a touch off key.

I'm no longer in reality considering what I'm doing, so to speak.

I begin to speak lower again and argue that it's simply my dream, and I'm on top of factors. With one flick of his hand he lifts me about 6 ft up into the air.

He's the usage of telekinesis on me! That's my factor!

I hold close there in the sky, powerless.

I can't pass in any respect, and I am even though absolutely lucid.

I'm not losing recognition and I'm nonetheless very a good deal aware of what's taking place, and (I concept) on top of things. He places me down gently and goes without delay to offer an cause behind that it's now not definitely absolutely everyone's dream, however that we're all right here collectively in this region.

I'm amazed.

I don't apprehend what to say, and so once I get positioned down on the ground I bypass walking. I walk out of the city and right into a wasteland place. I don't have a aim for wherein I'm going at this issue I simply need to get back to somewhere 'ordinary' something which means.

Dissolving the dream u . S . A .

At this stage in the dream I'm blown away. I don't realize what's occurring any extra and I do a few fact checks to make clearly positive that I'm dreaming, and I am of course. I can though fly, I can notwithstanding the fact that increase timber and create cash but for a few reason lower again there inside the town I modified into overpowered.

It's now not like I became awaiting it both, I was virtually on pinnacle of things of my feelings, thoughts and ideals and however I in reality couldn't do a little thing. Strange. That's in no way came about earlier than, but it have become about to get higher..

I'm inside the barren location clearing and I go searching me. I enjoy humbled, sort of like

I've without a doubt come out of a deep meditation session and I'm feeling 'in love' with the area. I revel in high-quality! But it's greater than exceptional, and from this element on a few aspect that I've never experienced in advance than started out to happen.

I commenced to experience EVERYTHING. All at once. But 10 instances higher, larger and similarly effective

When I say 'the whole lot', I imply it like this:

Imagine for a 2d the remaining time you laughed

till you cried, and you felt intensely glad or cherished

Now recall the last time you orgasmed

or had intercourse

Now the closing time you've got been heartbroken

or out of place a chum/member of the family/pet, a few problem

Now don't forget the final time you felt in fact happy or cherished

The feeling of water in opposition for your body while you swim in the sea, the sensation of ice cold water as you drink on a warm summers day, and the whole lot in among.

Now believe ALL of those subjects, all the ones moments of emotional price, ALL AT ONCE, except x100.

Imagine feeling the intense satisfaction, the pain, and it's all mixed collectively and amplified via about 10 instances. It's overpowering and I can't do something with it, aside from simply permit it arise and absolutely deliver in to this enjoy.

I fall again, powerless and overwhelmed and lightly drift above the ground, looking up on the sky. The sky is not a mixture of blue vicinity and clouds but is definitely a white glowing mild.

Everywhere I look is white. It's certainly white energy, all spherical me. It's no longer the equal type of white light that you'd assume, it's extra like being underwater and SURROUNDED thru the mild. You can't have a observe it or attention on it as it IS your reputation.

It's everything you're aware about and you could't awareness on any character part of it, as it's satisfactory ONE thing.

I don't even try to recognition on it and as an alternative attention at the feelings surging through me. Those extreme feelings are although dashing through me at a ordinary rate. They don't sluggish down, they actually live there constantly. It doesn't harm as such, it honestly feels extremely good. Like I've been given a huge, powerful strength and it's overcoming my whole frame.

I'm abruptly aware about the whole thing. I feel my frame napping in mattress, I experience the limitless possibilities of dream adventures round me. I see excellent white power however I'm privy to loads greater than that. I can genuinely revel in the whole thing, and I can see my whole existence's memories laid out in the front of me.

It's like they're simply all being shown to me on the identical time, form of like in case you have been in a room with one hundred TV displays all playing incredible films on the equal time. Normally that might be not feasible to reputation on, however in this dream I can also need to understand and provide interest to all of them at the same time.

I revel in my increase as someone, I see my maximum lovable recollections. Some that I didn't even realise I had. I feel like I'm crying, however it's no longer in reality crying due to the opposite feelings and power surging through me. Whatever this country changed into, it felt without a doubt great and I by no means preferred it to give up.

It's like I'd transcended the whole thing I knew to be actual, and I modified into loose.

This became the number one time I'd dissolved the dream state like this, and I am now going to try it each time I lucid dream. I speak to this dream as 'lucid transcendence'.

Notes about the dream:

The night time time earlier than I'd had some drinks with a chum, so it may had been a 'REM rebound' lucid dream. I began the dream commonly and feature emerge as lucid by means of manner of manner of doing the 'finger thru the palm' truth check. As the dream superior I built on the stability with the aid of grounding myself and respiratory deeply.

So it changed into pretty immoderate but searching once more, that became the start of my slightly more immoderate lucid dreams. From then on I've been having hundreds more of these types of goals, quite regularly.

They not best make me wake up feeling excited about life and energised, however they open my eyes as to the opportunities of this international and the idea that there can be plenty greater available that we simply can't experience or superb as humans.

Setting up your room for lucid dreaming

You can do some matters to the actual room you sleep in to make it much more likely you'll lucid dream. This is what I called lucid prepping and it's very clean. There are some number one elements which we'll move over now:

Chapter 8: Incense And Aromas

Incense and the way your room smells can be very critical. The smells we revel in do topics to our thoughts and emotional u . S ., so for lucid dreaming you're aiming for a cushty kingdom.

Not nice that, you're aiming for a snug however additionally aware u . S . A The brilliant aromas for this are Lavender and Jasmine. These aromas will help you now not great loosen up however moreover be in the proper recognition country for lucid dreaming.

The notable factor to do is really to get a few incense sticks and burn them proper before bed so the aroma is all over the room. Combine this with a lavender pillow spray and also you'll go together with the waft right off, with greater risk of being lucid!

Temperature and smart domestic devices

You can simply use smart gadgets in your private home that will help you turn out to be lucid. Not anyone has those, so if you don't have smart domestic gadgets then feel free to skip this phase!

Use clever alarms for the Wake Back To Bed approach

If you've been searching for to lucid dream for some time, you're probably familiar

with the Wake Back To Bed (WBTB) approach

. This is where you wake yourself throughout REM sleep, after which move again to sleep, with your thoughts unsleeping and alert. Smart home devices can honestly make this approach an entire lot much less complicated.

If you've have been given a Google Home or an Amazon Alexa, you could without a doubt effects set an alarm for a positive time. And even better, you could pick what wakes you up, be it your preferred tune, the radio, or in reality the voice of your tool.

So for the WBTB method, you may set your smart alarm for 2-three hours in advance than you would typically awaken (as that is at the same time as you're maximum possibly to be in REM sleep).

Hold on a minute even though, truely this is nobody-of-a-kind from every one-of-a-kind alarm? Nope. There's one function that makes smart alarms top notch for lucid dreamers: The voice controls.

With the WBTB technique, you don't need to interrupt out from mattress to show off your alarm. In reality, you need to avoid moving your body if you can help it.

So even as remarkable alarms require a few form of movement to reveal them off, you can certainly name out on your smart device to save you the alarm. This manner, your frame remains prepared to fall once more to sleep, whilst your thoughts is wakeful, alert, and organized to get lucid!

Use your clever devices to do fact tests

Part of the fun of clever domestic gadgets is looking them ridiculous questions and seeing what they answer. But a no longer-so-ridiculous query to invite is 'am I dreaming?'

Depending on what tool you've got were given, you'll possibly get considered one in every of two answers: 'no' or 'sorry, I don't comprehend that one'.

Either manner, each time you ask your device whether or no longer or no longer or no longer you're dreaming, you apprehend you're going to get the equal response. This is a remarkable way to do

a fact test

, in spite of the truth that it does make you sound a bit mad.

Doing everyday reality assessments is one of the fine methods to enhance your possibilities of turning into lucid. They additionally assist you apprehend on the equal time as you virtually do emerge as lucid.

Let's say you ask the equal question, 'am I dreaming?, out loud in a dream. If you're not met with the identical voice or response as your clever device typically offers you, you'll apprehend your lucidity.

Using clever temperature manipulate to stimulate sleep levels

Some clever home gadgets hook up in your heating or aircon tool, making it splendid easy to elevate or decrease the temperature in your property.

If you could use your clever home tool to change the temperature to your room at a high quality time, this could help you lucid dream.

We discover it only to fall asleep in a temperature that's no longer too warm temperature, and not too cold, so for the majority of the night time, your home's ordinary temperature is fantastic.

But in case you really need to make lucid dreaming that bit easier, you could use your clever domestic device to elevate the temperature a hint in the early hours of morning (this is at the same time as you're much more likely to revel in REM sleep).

Vivid desires have frequently been related to warmer temperatures, therefore why we frequently wake up from desires in a sweat. So if the temperature in your bedroom increases a bit after you're already asleep, your mind might be introduced inside the path of awakening, and also you'll discover your dreams turn out to be extra vibrant or even lucid.

You want to get the temperature stability absolutely proper even though, in any other case you'll each no longer dream, or in reality awaken because of the truth you're too heat. It takes a piece of exercise to examine the best balance.

Use smart devices to simulate daylight

As nicely because of the reality the alarms that come constructed into maximum smart domestic devices, there are also cause built clever alarms. Smart alarms wake you up with a sunlight simulation, so you enjoy as in spite of the reality that you've arisen with the solar.

Why should you need that? Because it's masses nicer and less difficult to awaken feeling like you've finished so evidently, with the solar, in vicinity of with a few shrill and traumatic alarm tone.

Ive in my view been the use of a dawn alarm clock for an wonderful few months and the distinction it makes is massive. It seems like you're just slowly and peacefully waking up, in location of being THROWN far from mattress through an annoying alarm.

Plus, sunlight hours simulations assist you sync your inner body clock together with your manner of existence, in order that regardless of even as you're getting your sleep, you enhance the great of your sleep and sense nicely rested and energised at a few degree in the day.

To be honest even though, you only actually need a sunrise alarm in case you don't already get daylight on your room. The one-of-a-kind time you may want it's miles if you're waking up BEFORE the solar in fact rises virtually.

I for example, commonly awaken at about five that is in advance than the solar rises most of the three hundred and sixty five days. So for this I use a sunrise alarm clock however one among a kind instances of the three hundred and sixty five days or if the sunrise is BEFORE five, I clearly set an audio alarm on my cellular telephone and awaken that way.

Many humans are often get rid of lucid dreaming because they enjoy worn-out after trying techniques similar to the WILD and

WBTB. But with a sunlight alarm clock, that comes on at something time you choose, you obtained't enjoy the tiring results of lucid dreaming.

There's furthermore the fact that a comfortable mind-set is high to getting lucid. Waking as much as an worrying alarm noise can placed you in a burdened temper for the entire day, but with a clever daylight hours alarm, you'll experience excellent approximately going to sleep and waking up.

Chapter 9: What Are Lucid Dreams?

Lucid dreaming, that is the act of dreaming and being conscious that one is dreaming, has been spherical for a long term. Lucid dreams are noted inside the writings of Aristotle. Other fantastic philosophers have furthermore written approximately them. Some evidence shows that even the Egyptians can also moreover have used lucid dreaming techniques. Evidence that lucid dreaming turned into used to prepare for dying is located in Egyptian and Tibetan books of the useless. It is likewise recognized that ancient yogis used lucid dreaming for astral tour and that Buddhist monks practiced dream yoga to find out their inner self.

WHY THE LUCID DREAM?

More importantly, why can we do it? Although it may appear banal, this question is vital if we need to get the maximum out of lucid dreaming. If we ask ourselves why frequently sufficient, we're capable of subsequently discover the idea desire that emerge as hidden until now.

This is precisely why we must ask this important and reputedly clean query. It allows us to discover what lies below our recognition. It is the begin of lucid dreaming, a workout that permits us to go into the unconscious and aware geographical regions to recover additives of ourselves.

Concentration is the vital aspect to lucid dreaming. To benefit lucidity in an altered state, most of the capabilities important for it require you to be aware about your sensations and use them to select out the states of consciousness you are in. You can then manipulate how you have got interaction in the ones states. All of this requires a smooth and targeted technique. This form of attention starts offevolved offevolved with articulating why you are doing this.

Whether you are new to lucid dreaming or an expert practitioner, take a 2d to ask yourself: Why are you lucid? Your dreams are much less in all likelihood to deliver you the rewards and effects you choice. Your direction may be extra centered if you apprehend your motivations for embarking on this adventure. Another key to achievement is to have a clean vision of your adventure.

There are many superficial answers that can be located while you ask why. It is essential to delve deeper into them. Do you aspire to have unique abilities? Do you choice extra pleasure in existence? Perhaps it is terrific to look for motivation in improving yourself-picture. Before you focus your interest on the what, spend an entire lot of time expertise the why. It takes energy and time to find out your real desires and align them with the desires that will help you acquire them.

It is likewise a dynamic query. Over time, the solution can also exchange. The motivations, goals and motives that force us these days may also lose their stress day after today, a 12 months or a decade from now. Our why will alternate as we expand and study, simply as our priorities, ideals and lives alternate.

My first exploration of lucid dreaming become for entertainment. When I grow to be in my twenties, I ought to have replied "For fun and to escape from everyday existence" while asked why I lucid dreamed. But as I determined out more approximately the arena of lucid dreaming, I observed out there was masses extra to it than I notion. I decided that lucid dreaming allowed me to connect to a deeper part of my Self, similarly to understand its dream worldwide. I commenced out out dreaming of escaping, however ended up dreaming of staying with myself and becoming extra complete.

WHAT TO EXPECT FROM A LUCID DREAM

Acid goals can provoke a massive variety of bodily sensations. All of these sensations are regular and not unusual. The maximum common sensation is vibrations. They can range from a slight tingling to the feeling of the body dissolving or falling aside. These sensations may be alarming, however they are not some thing to fear approximately. They endorse that you are becoming aware about the gadget of falling asleep. Once you loosen up, they'll disappear. Take a have a take a look at the dream enjoy I had:

As I go to sleep, I enjoy the vibrations that commonly get up as soon as I realize I am going to have an out-of-body dream-like enjoy. I awaken and find myself in my room. Everything seems slower and I suspect I am dreaming. When I search around my room, I count on I is probably sleepwalking. Everything is gradual and although actual. I'm afraid my roommates will phrase I'm taking walks round my house, but I determine it's well worth the danger and head to the rest room to appearance within the mirror. . . . .

Although I actually have had many lucid dreams earlier than this, this situation suggests how real the lucid dream enjoy may be. It is important to be open to the surprising and to be privy to what you experience in lucid desires. These thoughts are especially relevant on your physical sensations and your environment. You can evaluate the dreaming and waking versions of each.

UNDERSTAND YOUR BODY

Lucid dream research may be scary and perplexing. They can also reason lucid wants to emerge as terrible or quit suddenly if they may be now not understood. You can regulate the outcome and course of the dream thru exciting your frame.

Certain sensations can be used to provoke lucid goals or distinct out-of-body testimonies. A lucid dream or out-of-body experience can be delivered approximately through manner of the usage of buzzing sounds. These sounds may be heard at some point of sleep paralysis or before. This form of dream is regularly associated with paralysis, hypnotic hallucinations, and the feeling of floating or falling. These varieties of dreams will now not be as alarming in case you don't forget that they are common.

REALISM

A man or woman generally exams the environment at the same time as she or he starts offevolved to find out a dream. Normal lucid dreams incorporate a decrease diploma of realism than fact. The dream can also moreover incorporate unrealistic characters or inconceivable physics.

In instances in which humans have lucid desires without-of-body reviews, realism will boom to each exclusive level. Out-of-body critiques can bring about a heightened awareness that the person is dreaming or traveling to some exceptional measurement of reality. Out-of-body desires frequently have extra detail than ordinary lucid desires. Many dreamers keep in mind that out-of-body opinions are actual three-d research.

Experiments on out-of-frame reviews show that they exceed fashionable truth tests, indicating that they'll be greater than simply lucid dreams. The following dream come to be tested thru me, and I provided it at the begin of this financial catastrophe.

I flip my toilet mild on and off and it definitely works flawlessly. This leads me to don't forget that I am sleepwalking. I observe that the entirety is slightly inexperienced when I appearance in the reflect. I see my footwear as I stroll down the stairs foremost out of doors. I vicinity my footwear so I can wake up the following morning and be conscious that I am sleepwalking. I pass outdoor and see the splendid stars and supernovas. I wander round for some time and then lose lucidity. Then, I sincerely have an prolonged sleep. I wake up and apprehend that my shoes are not located surprisingly. I furthermore understand that it's miles about fifteen ranges out of doors. This would probably have made me awaken if my snoozing clothes were but on.

Although I believed the dream modified into real, it modified into now not viable to create any cease give up result that could allow me to attach the dream with truth. According to theories, our thoughts creates worlds just like the simplest we sleep in on the same time as we experience an out-of-body revel in. Many times, there can be a portal. Literally, it's miles a window or door in the dream that we are able to go through to go into a particular worldwide.

Although it is not appeared why these desires appear more real than super forms of lucid or lucid dreams, it is viable that the mind area that gives with prolonged-term reminiscences and motive stays energetic in the course of sleep. One concept is that goals may be interconnected with an exchange reality or shape of reality, referred to as the astral. No recollect what the purpose, many those who revel in out-of-frame sports additionally experience vibrations and have auditory and seen hallucinations.

AWARENESS

THE ROUTE TO THE "BEYOND".

Being aware about dreaming can mean many stuff to wonderful humans. It is once in a while called lucid dreaming.

When a dreamer reaches a high quality degree of attention in a dream usa, they may bear in mind themselves to have had an "out-of-body" enjoy. Some people describe themselves as aware on the same time as touring via a number of realities beyond the acknowledged senses of time in an astral country. What is the boundary amongst waking fact, passive dreaming, and lucid dreaming?

These variations can only be made if we first recognize reputation. What exactly is awareness? What is awareness and the manner is it one in each of a kind from the thoughts? These ideas have to be understood an awesome manner to discover altered dream states in a vast manner.

In the clinical network, research on consciousness is a novelty. Until presently, it turn out to be difficult to recognize attention. We normally have a tendency to confuse recognition with concept due to the reality we understand it as such. That is why we overlook the anomaly of lucid dreaming or extraordinary techniques of exploring the past our thoughts: focus is a bodily phenomenon.

Consciousness manifests as consciousness, alertness and interest. These states may be skilled internally and may most effective be professional by using the use of one character. They are simplest evidenced externally with the useful resource of the behavior they produce. This is sufficient for practical features.

This is a rather immoderate implication. If focus can't be externally professional or tested, then my exceptional truth about my very very very own popularity is that it isn't always possible for me to recognize the fact. I can't be positive of some thing beyond that. I do no longer recognize in case you, the reader, are conscious. I can only offer the gain of the doubt.

Current theories on the origins and evolution of consciousness recognition on each the observer and the located. Tony Nader is a neuroscientist and researcher who's moreover a leader in Transcendental Meditation. He believes that to be conscious, a few factor have to have critical traits.

Must be capable of observe.

He need to have visible himself.

It's basically a chicken and egg problem. To be privy to myself, I first ought to observe myself or my attention. To be aware, however, I have to first be aware to look at and test my attention.

CONSCIOUSNESS IS PHYSICAL

Many philosophical and summary techniques to consciousness display the manner it develops inside the mind and in our surroundings. These techniques are handiest one view of methods attention can specific itself. The physical approach to know-how attention is more essential than the philosophical and precis ones. It can display plenty about how interest arose and what it takes to revel in it. Our facts of attention draws at the physiological and natural basis of popularity in methods which are as great as they will be unexpected.

The human mind gets sensory records in 250 milliseconds. On not unusual, it takes 30 to 50 milliseconds to deliver stimuli to the mind, followed by means of a hundred fifty milliseconds to method them before they obtain our consciousness. The normal activation of synapses, additionally called cognition, is what we name recognition. Neuroscientists and philosophers disagree on whether or now not this is similar to recognition or cognition.

Although it can appear that that is an automated system and that we are virtually experiencing what it's miles, what's in reality taking area behind the scenes is more like a computer show walking at sixty frames in line with 2nd, giving us the illusion of seeing a non-forestall picture.

The proof that physical memories can affect cognizance is overwhelming. Changes in how the frame functions, including what you eat, what you drink and what you do with it, collectively with physical trauma and strain, can reason hormonal modifications that bring about reactions inside the mind which might be then skilled as interest.

The opposite is real: recognition could have an impact on bodily states. As the vintage pronouncing goes, trade the way you observe and the belongings you see will trade. Many global traditions take delivery of as true with that exchange starts offevolved offevolved with the spirit. Then the thoughts techniques the information to create the responses in the frame. This perception is supported with the useful resource of many cultures, each historic and present day-day. The equal is true in recent times if we alternative the word spirit for interest. Changes in attention can alter the hormonal balances within the thoughts, which in turn affects the complete body.

Studying focus may be described as analyzing a map made with magic ink. When the hidden image is illuminated, its hidden because of this that is located. The mind's oxygen consumption can be used as a biomarker to assist researchers take a look at awareness. If the thoughts consumes extra oxygen in certain areas, it approach that those areas have emerge as more energetic. This evaluation famous that one in all a type areas of the thoughts are concerned in superb responsibilities, and that consciousness is based upon on many factors.

Although we can not see cognizance, we're able to observe neural interest and oxygen utilized by the brain in a manner that suggests that cognizance is occurring. We can select out out styles in neural pastime and begin to apprehend the man or woman of reputation.

It is vital to do not forget that reputation does now not are looking for advice from the mind, the senses or a specific u . S . A . Of hobby. External elements, which incorporates the functioning of our brain and senses, may have an effect on our focus or the mind or perceptions we make. We can regulate reputation depending on how we engage with our senses, how our mind functions, or how we alternate our kingdom of focus, however interest is a part unto itself, self-contained as a state of focus that is have come to be on whilst conscious or have emerge as off while unconscious.

Understanding the techniques wherein outside forces can modify recognition is handiest part of records its malleability. How subjects are placed out modifications the improvement of attention. We brief absorb new subjects and abilties on the identical time as we first examine them. Learning takes place in the aware mind. After information is processed, it's miles stored in memory. This reminiscence lives in our unconscious. This is called implicit cognition. Implicit reminiscence is a aggregate of cognition, notion and reminiscence. It affects conduct however isn't always conscious. A traditional example of implicit cognition is that we take into account a way to ride a bicycle. The memory of the method is saved inside the decrease lower back of our mind, so while we start the use of, recollections of the frame automatically come to the fore.

Chapter 10: States Of Consciousness

There are three states of consciousness that may be found in genuinely anyone:

Awake: You are unsleeping, alert, cell and engaged for your every day sports activities.

Dreaming: You are most probable experiencing REM sleep. You might also have a dream or a simulated reality enjoy at some point of sleep.

Deep sleep: While you are not conscious or dreaming, deep sleep allows you to be aware of mind and feel lucid. Deep sleep can motive sleep paralysis, further to different out-of-frame memories.

In each of the states, an impairment also can occur in which popularity does no longer function nicely or collapses. This does not imply that the character is unconscious or conscious. It simplest technique that there may be an altered country of interest that abilities in a particular manner than might be expected while surely conscious. Below are a few examples of altered states.

Anesthesia is at the same time as a person is speedy subconscious and is given a chemical substance that motives his or her mind to go into a nap u . S . A ..

The u . S . Of being locked in: Total paralysis of the body that makes one not capable of flow. This is while the character feels trapped in his or her body. It is just like sleep paralysis, or other paralysis reviews in which the man or woman is aware about sensations.

Minimally aware: Although the mind remains capable of responding to three stimuli, it isn't always in a country of complete awareness.

Vegetative country: A person is completely unresponsive (as even though vain). This sleep united states of america is just like an man or woman's wakefulness.

Coma: An man or woman is not able to experience the cycles of waking, drowsing or dreaming. He is locked right into a unmarried country of being this is an lousy lot much less aware than his minimally conscious us of a.

There are many types of altered states of attention, that could purpose cognizance in particular techniques. Here are a few examples of the tales one ought to have whilst in altered states of reputation:

Drug-added on hypnotic memories: When certain hallucinogenic drugs are administered, mind functioning may be altered to create special states of focus. Perceptions, notion styles and emotions can be notably altered in contrast to what's skilled while not the use of the drug. However, this doesn't necessarily advise that the person is subconscious. Many times, the person can preserve complete reputation even on the identical time as using those materials.

Lucid goals: A individual can experience lucid desires while they will be asleep. This is after they turn out to be conscious that they are dreaming. This does now not always propose that the dreamer enters the dream. However, it's far feasible that she or he does.

Sleepwalking: Although now not regularly remembered, an man or woman may be conscious that he or she can skip in a sleep nation.

Hypnosis is a country of cognizance wherein the person is capable of see outdoor affects and remains wide awake.

As you can see, attention can exchange during the day. It's not pretty much how conscious we're, however also about how we perceive our truth and engage at a essential diploma with it. Interestingly, our hobby is right away related to how our frame reacts to the area spherical it, which includes our sleep cycles.

MODULATION OF LEARNING AND BRAIN AWARENESS

Certain areas of the mind understand and method out of doors stimuli. This facts is processed to create a fact that makes feel. Reality isn't what we certainly see. We great apprehend a processed and tailor-made illustration of the records. It can take in to 1 / four of a 2nd before we are aware about what we see. Before we come to be aware of information, some areas of the thoughts perceive it first. Consciousness most effective takes place while some other region of the brain becomes aware of the facts.

The a part of the mind accountable for regulating wakefulness is referred to as the reticular formation. This place also controls interest. Damage to it is able to bring about coma. The reticular formation gets all sensory data earlier than it's far processed by means of the use of the use of unique components of the mind. The thoughts moreover has one of a kind areas which may be chargeable for specific factors of consciousness. The easy bodily capabilities that regulate homeostasis are controlled with the useful resource of the hypothalamus. The center of the self, or what we recognize because the ego, is managed by manner of way of the amygdala and the midbrain. The cortex, moreover known as the autobiographical self or autobiographical self, is language, speech and reminiscence.

The mind creates a simulation of the non-stop reality developing a shielding impact. This is because of the truth the thoughts takes time to machine all of the statistics. The thoughts creates records from what it can't obtain from the surroundings to present us a non-prevent revel in in recognition. Individuals with certain mind illnesses or lesions may moreover experience a cinematic view of time that slows down and feature moments of notion in desire to a non-save you go along with the flow. This loss of time can also be due to other elements, which include mind harm or traumatic sports.

The unconscious thoughts preprocesses the aware enjoy we've inside the path of the day (information we aren't but privy to), so there can be continuously an issue of ourselves that isn't always obvious. This unconscious area controls an crucial part of our experience. Lucid dreaming is even as we actively try to be aware about what we're seeing. If the subconscious thoughts does no longer want us to come to be privy to the goals, we will never be able to gather this. Lucid dreaming techniques create a courting with the subconscious to come to be greater aware of the subconscious cloth in goals.

CONSCIOUSNESS IS PSYCHOSPIRITUAL

Another difficulty of attention is having an ego, or a experience of self, that takes region within the history. Even in case you don't keep in mind who or what you're as someone, focus is answerable for shaping your self-idea. The equal self-generated recognition is obvious in how we define ourselves. For example, identification, form, nationality or repute.

Real recognition, which extends past the experience of self and is important in your fashionable view of fact, is every other element of reputation. Real attention is your mind, emotions, plans, desires, intentions, wishes and feelings. These are your moves, or the way you appear what you want most. Real recognition isn't always tied to who you're as an person. Instead, it's far an expression and manifestation of what the Self maximum goals.

The critical detail to remember is that your sense of self (or ego) is remarkable part of who you simply are. There are elements of you that you do no longer understand which can be critical on your dream enjoy. You are much more likely to awaken to the deeper factors of yourself if you can create a communicate among them. It is often a exquisite deal higher to permit the subconscious manual us into hobby in a dream than to stress it. The unconscious is what controls the dream international. The unconscious is what leads us to lucidity. It brings the subconscious cloth to interest.

CONSCIOUSNESS IS A PHILOSOPHY

Although the terminology used to give an explanation for interest might also moreover exchange counting on how others define it, in popular the ability to be conscious and aware, in addition to the ability to evaluate the environment, are the most critical elements of being conscious. Understanding that I am in a feature and able to examine the surroundings is an critical factor of focus is important. Unconsciously, I can be aware of some factor but no longer be able to consciously examine it.

What is the element of all this? These thoughts are the cornerstones of lucid dreaming. And because interest is not similar to wakefulness, we're able to revel in empowered and capable of explore our dream worlds. Being aware, alert and attentive even while dozing enhances the capacity to lucid dream.

On the alternative hand, the subconscious without a doubt consists of the whole lot that isn't aware, but impacts the conscious mind. The unconscious includes ideas together with early critiques that have caused the character and forgotten recollections. These aren't normally available for inspection. Some of those recollections may be accessed with the resource of converting our interest. Some of these memories can be accessed via way of converting our awareness.

The Unconscious does no longer exist within the mind; the conscious is simplest aware of what the subconscious is aware of.

-FRENCH JEFFREY

The unconscious is not itself subconscious. We are genuinely no longer aware of it. Only we will understand that there may be a few aspect interior us of which we are unaware. However, the truth that we're consciously privy to some thing does now not imply that we are not further or extra aware of it unconsciously. Carl G. Jung, a former pupil of Freud, and ostensibly the real so-referred to as depth psychologist, believed that the subconscious became more energetic in shaping who we're. Jung believed that the subconscious changed into accountable for our attention, our ego and our revel in of self.

It is important to apprehend that our subconscious is part of the exploration of dreams. Dream evaluations can help us deliver the subconscious into our aware thoughts. Lucid dreaming and dream evaluation allow us to engage with our unconscious to find out greater approximately the symbols and archetypes in our dreams, and to discover its desires and desires. Interacting with the ones archetypes leads us to a more attention of our right self.

Someday we are able to understand how our brains have interaction with our senses and complexes to discover the arena spherical them. We can already understand humans's mind the usage of new technology at the same time as now not having to invite. Brain styles may be used to determine what is going on inside the brain, with out the need to speak to the man or woman. These styles may be diagnosed the usage of positron emission tomography (PET scanning). Although the technology remains very primitive, it's far promising.

Researchers are though trying to determine out what makes focus actual. Is it possible to recreate attention? How can we understand the subjective research all people have? How are we able to apprehend our private enjoy close to that of others? No one is aware about the answer.

However, it seems apparent that creativeness is part of subjective revel in. The energy of imagination is what makes recognition and self-interest possible. It is viable to rouse to our goals the use of imagination.

Awareness

How to put together your dream

At first appearance, it would appear that lucid dreaming is a substantially easy functionality to comprehend. All we should do to have a lucid imaginative and prescient is simply to dream. How are we able to acquire it? It is as smooth as identifying the differences among dreaming and fact. However, that is a tough task for max human beings. Why? Why? Because our functionality to make rational observations is very limited in our dream kingdom. It is critical to increase the capability to lucid dream thru manner of being aware of your surroundings at some point of the day.

It appears that through increasing our reputation in the course of the day, we're able to growth our recognition in the course of goals. This will make it less complicated to apprehend that we're dreaming. Let's have a look at this.

Chapter 11: What Is Awareness?

I regularly discover myself zoning out sooner or later of the day. I can power spherical town and arrive at my vacation spot, no longer even know-how how or what I became listening to at the radio. This takes area due to the fact my mind is in a trance-like state, which I remember is to address boredom while using. It is also viable to tune out to avoid uninteresting or regular sports activities. We all experience the ones moments of absent-mindedness often an afternoon.

While it may seem alarming to think that we're all in a trance, there are some benefits. It does not advise we should be targeted at the things we do no longer like and we're capable of skip some vicinity else on the equal time as doing the ones responsibilities. We also can escape and plan things that may not be inside the front of our eyes, or have mini-adventures and fantasies on the identical time as concentrating.

However, this usa has some drawbacks. One of them is that we lose sight of the vital topics spherical us. Apart from the plain dangers, inclusive of the possibility of getting into an twist of destiny whilst riding, we additionally aren't able to be aware of all or part of what is taking location inside the second. It is viable to disconnect from the actual global. This can be beneficial in certain situations, collectively with trauma, but in normal life, these periods of desensitization can cause us to overlook the most crucial subjects.

Lucid dreaming and the attention practices that assist it can help us benefit the opportunity of dissociation. We are more concerned, unsleeping and succesful to take part in our lives while conscious, in addition to whilst dreaming.

Our capacity to talk with the subconscious improves as we end up more aware and worried in our each day lives. The unconscious can show us symbolic photographs and messages that we are able to recognize. The subconscious can take over within the dream space, causing our focus to enter a symbolic international that is normally unknown to us. If we do not practice recognition training to come to be extra aware about this transition, we will become surely absorbed with the aid of the usage of the unconscious worldwide and lose sight of what we're truly dreaming.

MINDFULNESS

Mindfulness is one of the super approaches to teach the thoughts for lucid dreaming. It's no wonder that two of the region's oldest lucid dreaming traditions, Egypt and Tibet, furthermore have the most massive mindfulness and meditation practices. Modern studies has examined this connection: Researchers placed a excellent correlation in lucid dreamers who've been capable of lucid dream and those who had practiced mindfulness training.

Consciousness method to be aware. It is the act of being attentive to what you are proper away privy to, so that you can see what's actual. Mindfulness schooling is exactly this. Mindfulness education is the exercise and art of listening to the triumphing moment. It allows you to pay extra interest to what also can appear everyday, further to teach your mind to be greater flexible. Mindfulness workout will boom your functionality to be privy to anything you pick out.

What makes Mindfulness art work?

Mindfulness education improves mind connections. The mind creates neural connections while we attention our interest on an object or concept. The mind's capability to alternate suggests that it improves its capacity to approach facts associated with what it considers critical. This is some other example of the brain's fantastic adaptive capabilities.

The body also can gain from mindfulness. The body is an virtual and chemical verbal exchange device. The thoughts sends electric powered impulses to the body, which is probably then transferred to the nerves. These chemical signs can then tour to other nerves. These electric powered and chemical indicators become being translated into motion of part of your frame. Some people believe that the gaps a number of the nerves can also store chemical substances. These gaps will also be responsible for trauma, ache or one among a type illnesses. If we cognizance on specific areas of the frame, we're capable of direct electrical and chemical impulses to the ones regions. This will enhance sign transmission and growth the mind's interest of those components. This will can help you release any trauma or pain this is stored in your body.

HOW TO PRACTICE MINDFULNESS

There are techniques of mindfulness that may be specially useful in getting prepared for lucid dreaming. The first is mindfulness meditation. Another is fact checking. Let's take a look at every.

Mindfulness meditation

Mindfulness meditation wants to prevent wondering. This allows energy generally spent on busy questioning to be directed in the direction of interest. People mistakenly trust that the intention of mindfulness meditation is to haven't any mind. This is wrong. Mindfulness meditation asks that we allow thoughts to spread and be open to without a doubt receive any feedback. Over time, your mind will learn how to be much less associated with wandering thoughts through running in the direction of non-attachment.

Traditional mindfulness meditation includes lying down bypass-legged along side your lower back right away and comfortable. The intellectual manner is surely to permit thoughts and emotions unfold as you take a look at them. You have to not pressure your thoughts or decide them. Be aware of your mind and let them waft.

Reality check

Reality checking may be considered a fundamental shape of lucid dreaming. This exercise is a easy manner to invite your self if the dream is actual. However, it requires some steps.

Be aware of your environment. This manner being aware of your environment, at the side of the smells and enjoy of devices. Cell phones, watches, and your arms are right examples of items you can focus on.

Next, awareness on the object you have got selected and search for any strangeness. Then ask yourself, "Am I dreaming?". This is similar to reciting a mantra. It is a repetition of terms that brings interest.

These types of reality assessments need to be executed often enough so that you can look carefully on the devices to your desires and ask yourself, "Am I dreaming?" Just as you do within the waking realm. You will regularly look at unusual residences in dreams in case you pay attention to items closely. For instance, your hand can also have seven palms in area of five. This will assist you understand that you are absolutely asleep and dreaming.

This technique can be improved through identifying the versions amongst dream and waking truth at once after waking from a dream. Observe the desires you have got had, inclusive of sounds, photographs, and physical sensations. Compare them to the real international. You can benefit a better degree of cognizance in every the waking and dream kingdom in case you get into the dependancy of evaluating the dream worldwide with the actual global.

QUALITY REST

Everyone merits an first-rate night time's sleep. We regularly wake up exhausted. However, once in a while we do now not get to sleep whilst we favored to, and we spend the night time time annoying or reeling from ache or soreness. This no longer best impacts our day, however additionally our ability and memory to don't forget our dreams. These competencies are important for lucid dreaming. Lucid dreaming is first-class feasible with an remarkable night time's sleep.

POOR SLEEP CAN HAVE NEGATIVE EFFECTS

Quality sleep can every now and then be interrupted with the useful resource of pressure and the complications of ordinary life. Our mind produces chemical modifications that would have an impact on reminiscence and cognition, similarly to hormones that have an impact on weight, weight loss program and temper. These outcomes might be noted in extra detail while we speak memory and dream don't forget in a later monetary ruin. The U.S. Military acknowledges the importance of suitable sleep and has made it obligatory for all defense force to get a tremendous type of hours of sleep.

IMPROVE YOUR SLEEP: FIRST-HAND EXPERIENCE

In the navy I located out about the negative outcomes of sleep deprivation and techniques to beautify sleep. In a sea of chaos, I worked prolonged hours on a Navy deliver. The art work changed into disturbing all day lengthy. Also, on a deliver there is lots of gadget and employees strolling throughout the clock. The supply's weapons tool made me feel my chest throbbing, and I should wake up among one and 3 within the morning.

A Navy deployment can last up to three hundred and sixty 5 days. Poor sleep can cause excessive mental and physical issues. Sleep disruptions can reason despair, aggression, confusion and weight benefit. Ferdinand Zizi and his research companion located that bad sleep can boom the risk of developing diabetes. For a healthful thoughts and frame, it is important to get precise, high-quality sleep.

Good sleep behavior are like learning a brand new device. It takes practice. Your sleep will decorate if you are affected character and curious to discover the exquisite equipment for you and feature the perseverance to be normal. You will feel extra awake, be greater inexperienced at night time and feature a better reminiscence to your each day existence and goals. It is essential to enlarge those property through establishing wholesome sleep conduct in a few unspecified time within the future of the day and night time time.

I modified into able to studies some very beneficial strategies while doing my army service. I in reality have persisted to use them at the same time as pursuing my dream career. These strategies can be divided into 3 commands: every day conduct together with exercise and vitamins, similarly to dietary supplements needed to useful resource rest and sleep.

DAILY HABITS TO PROMOTE SLEEP

What type of day could make you feel tired on the give up of the day? A day that includes lots of exercise, balanced vitamins and stimulating highbrow interest. It additionally consists of healthy control of feelings. These are the guidelines I've observed out via trial and errors. They may moreover additionally assist you growth your non-public sleep-selling conduct.

Being exhausted

New dad and mom, tourists, navy personnel and clearly everyone who works lengthy hours or has a annoying gadget may additionally tell you that being worn-out should make it hard to go to sleep brief. This is due to the reality pressure can bring about insomnia. Regular exercise can assist reduce cortisol levels, which in flip lets in the body and mind to loosen up, allowing you to sleep better. Cortisol (furthermore known as the strain hormone) is right now associated with sleep regulation and our circadian rhythm skills. You will sleep better if you reduce the amount of cortisol that is gift in the course of sleep.

Exercise

Regardless of your health degree, a top notch exercising will let you sleep higher via making your frame and mind physical exhausted. Exercise also can relieve strain and assist you worry a good deal less about your day. Although there may be lots scientific communicate approximately the effects of workout on sleep, it's far clean that exercising allows you doze off quicker and sleep higher. Light yoga is a terrific preference earlier than bedtime. It consists of deep respiration and stretching, which let you loosen up and nod off.

Diet

It is extensively identified that tryptophan may be an tremendous sleep food, much like Thanksgiving turkey. Because tryptophan will boom tiers of acetylcholine, this is an critical neurotransmitter for sleep. Serotonin and GABA are also proper for sleep. GABA, tryptophan and seeds are meals that comprise tryptophan. It is crucial to eat greater of those foods inside the path of the day and avoid consuming something earlier than bedtime. Eating healthy meals can also contribute to outstanding sleep.

While deployed inside the navy or at the battlefield, I regularly couldn't have healthy, delicious meals or make my personal choices. I needed to make do with what I had, at the same time as enhancing the fantastic of my sleep in one-of-a-kind techniques. I become able to discover nutrients and other dietary dietary supplements that made up the difference.

Supplements

You can use nutritional dietary supplements in combination with different techniques to help you grow to be extra unsleeping and aware at the same time as you sleep. Supplements allow you to sleep higher, on the same time as others will make you more wide conscious and alert inside the direction of sleep, increasing your chances of waking up in a dream. Although some humans don't forget dietary supplements to be a hoax for achieving lucid states of attention, many religious and non secular traditions have used nutritional dietary supplements and herbs. Today, many meals lack the nutrients needed to assist herbal sleep. Supplements can help your body advantage natural sleep states.

Melatonin is my sleep useful beneficial aid to help me get to bed on time. Melatonin is produced obviously via using the thoughts. It can be taken as a complement to help you doze off.

Niacin is my favored complement. It releases serotonin and a protein referred to as prostaglandin D2 (PGD2), that could be a snooze modulator. This helps us nod off.

Also notable sleep aids are 5-Hydroxytryptophan (five-HTP), cautiously related to serotonin, and St. John's Wort. They are moderate antidepressants that assist loosen up the mind and prepare for sleep.

Remember that vitamins and supplements want to only be used together along with your health practitioner's approval. They can pose a risk if not used efficiently. These and different nutritional nutritional dietary supplements can be discussed in greater element in Part five.

You can also lessen the amount of caffeine you devour at some level in the day to get an awesome night time time time's sleep. It sounds no longer viable, but it is possible. I reduce out coffee and strength beverages for a few months at the same time as serving within the Navy. This greatly improved the awesome of my sleep, my stamina and my regular health.

Chapter 12: A Route To Bed To Promote Good Sleep

Even if your ordinary has superior your chances of getting an incredible night time time's sleep, it's far the way you approach bedtime with a purpose to decide your success. This is what sets the level to your goals. You have to take care of your internal and outdoor surroundings a remarkable manner to have a healthy sleep cycle and practice having a pipe dream.

For your thoughts, create a stable location for snoozing

How the unconscious works and what it's far stays below debate. It seems that there are minds in our mind. As we stated earlier, the aware mind is what we expect with each day. It is likewise what we've in thoughts even as we consider our identification. The subconscious mind isn't part of our day by day cognizance. It thinks especially approximately survival. The unconscious is worried with preserving us secure and solid. It attracts our attention to what it thinks will preserve us secure and steady. Sometimes because of this the unconscious continues us awake, irrespective of the truth that our aware thoughts need to be asleep.

Perhaps you are pressured and your unconscious is detecting a threat which you can't defuse. Perhaps your creativeness is developing scary reminiscences, playing "what if" video games of possible futures, or retaining you alert to real or imagined threats. If this happens, you could locate it hard to go to sleep at night time time. You won't be actively worried about something, but the same problems are strolling to your records. The unconscious should now not distinguish. What's the solution?

How to calm the thoughts

A calm mind doesn't come from an area of "ifs" and "maybes." If your subconscious is sending you survival signs and symptoms, it's time to speak to your self, preserve a magazine and get out of the rut.

Meditation and interest schooling

Meditation teaches us that feelings and thoughts are regularly not as important as we assume. Meditation allows us to disconnect from our mind and quiet our busy minds to be extra effective in our lives. This consists of letting pass of our thoughts at bedtime.

Having the talk

If I lie down and my thoughts is racing, it takes me a while to nod off. That's while it's time for The Talk. When I turn to my personal thoughts, I write (or say) this: You understand it is essential to get sufficient sleep. These are the topics which can be bothering you proper now. List them. They are not important right now. They can't be regular urgently. No. They may be everyday day after today. We're stable until then. It's time to visit mattress proper now.

This allows to calm the mind via spotting your mind. For the subconscious to understand, we ought to talk or write sure terms.

The last a part of "The Talk" is powerful. If I say "It's time for bed!" out loud, I often yawn, get worn-out and go to sleep. Talking to oneself is a form of meditation. Clearing the mind is the essential issue to dreaming.

For the relaxation of your life, create a secure area for sleep

We set the degree for our goals via method of getting organized for mattress. This method that your bedroom and bedding need to be quiet and easy. Make awesome the distance is as uncluttered and smooth as feasible. Place devices in a manner that makes you experience happy and snug. Surround yourself with scents and textures that soothe your senses with out overwhelming them.

This is extra than developing a pleasing aesthetic. The issue to recall is the subconscious. Its reason is to keep your thoughts stable. Your brain can end up angry with litter, chaos and strain. Watch how an animal rests and arranges its bedding so it feels stable and stable. It's an great trouble.

Turn off the lighting

Put away your devices, too. Even if it makes you enjoy higher to be awake at night time time, your night time time moderate is not helping you sleep. Even the smallest quantity of slight can save you your thoughts from producing melatonin, the natural sleep aid. Your sleep hygiene will beautify if you have a darkened bed room.

Better sleep for all

You can decorate your sleep no matter your device, way of life, area or pressure degree. These equipment can help you gather a superb sleep surroundings. While no longer usually the fantastic, any improvement is a step within the proper direction.

It should be stated that I used those equipment in the route of my army deployment. Although I had a few sleepless nights, I ought to rate my stylish sleep great as remarkable. My functionality to sleep higher advanced notably.

I think so.

SLEEP PARALYSIS AND MEMORY

THE DOOR IS THE OBSTACLE

He lived by myself in an vintage house in Virginia at the identical time as walking as a navy mechanic at the night shift. Due to the strain of the time table and everyday paintings, I couldn't get as an awful lot sleep as I preferred. My roommates have to make loud noises for the duration of the day that might wake me from my normal sleep. Once, I idea my buddy jumped on my decrease once more and pinned my head to the mattress. Then, he started out blowing in my ears. This disturbed me and made it even greater scary. I couldn't skip due to his splendid energy. His respiratory intensified and made me pass extra difficult.

I changed into ultimately capable of unfastened myself and realized that I even have turn out to be on my own. I became asleep all the time and imagined everything.

I became terrified and started out discovering what had happened. I spent months getting to know and analyzing to discover what sleep paralysis have turn out to be and why it become taking place to me. I additionally positioned the way to address it so I must face my fears and regain manipulate of my dreams.

While this isn't intended to deter everyone from dreaming, it could be scary. Let's begin with the difficult thing.

Lucid desires can lead many human beings to come upon emotionally annoying subjects and images. These frightening pix are often followed thru an disability to move.

Sleep paralysis is a totally not unusual situation amongst lucid dreamers. You owe it to yourself to study greater earlier than you leap in.

WHAT IS SLEEP PARALYSIS?

It is the kingdom as a innocent duration of immobility, deriving from muscle paralysis, or atonia that takes area every night time as a herbal facet impact of dream sleep. This know-how can assist alleviate a number of the anxiety that may be skilled.

When our frame falls asleep, however we're partially conscious, this is referred to as sleep paralysis. This is because the mind transitions from speedy eye motion (REM) to non-speedy eye movement (NREM) sleep. The brain's transition from speedy eye movement (REM) to non-speedy eye movement (NREM) sleep often motives us to dream, however we're conscious that that is going on. The result can be hallucinations, which may additionally embody undesirable internet site site visitors or the sensation of being watched. Dreamers describe sleep paralysis as a feel of paralysis, the belief of a presence and the imaginative and prescient of terrifying creatures.

Although sleep paralysis may be scary, it's far regular. Rubin Naiman, Ph.D., is a psychologist and medical accomplice professor of medication. He is likewise the sleep and dream professional on the Andrew Weil Center for Integrative Medicine on the University of Arizona. He assured me that, despite the fact that it could be frightening, "sleep paralysis" is actually regular. In reality, our frame immobilizes us on the equal time as we sleep in order that we do not ought to act out our goals. This is what can get up if the mechanism fails. However, sleep paralysis is not to be feared. Sleepwalking has been linked to thoughts protrusion, according to analyze. Sam Kean stated, "Deep inside the reptilian mind is the pons, a centimeter-prolonged hump within the mind stem. The hump sends signs to the primate mind through which goals are initiated even as we go to sleep. The pons sends messages to the spinal twine underneath it sooner or later of desires. This produces chemical materials that numb the muscle groups. This short paralysis prevents nightmares and escape from the bed room.

Sleep paralysis is at the same time as we awaken and may hallucinate images approximately our out of doors environment. It is similar to an augmented fact for the mind.

People report feeling anxious and stressful after they fall asleep, regardless of what they see or concentrate. The reason can be hyperactivation of the amygdala, that is the worry middle of the mind. Sleep paralysis and amygdala activation may be the cause of nightmares or sleep paralysis.

WAYS TO PARTIALLY STOP SLEEPING

Researchers do not but recognize why some people revel in paralysis and others do now not. Research shows that sleep paralysis can be progressed if lucid dreaming strategies are used. Wake Back to Bed (WBTB), and Wake Induced Lucid Dreamings (WILD), lucid dreaming techniques that inspire practitioners to enjoy effects just like or mimicking sleep paralysis.

There isn't any manner to save you sleep paralysis. However, there are a few things you can do to lessen your risk.

Do now not sleep in your lower lower returned

Sleeping in regarded locations.

Do no longer take naps sooner or later of the day.

Get a few exercise within the path of the day.

Avoid pressure earlier than bedtime.

Avoid stimulants on the same time as snoozing.

To prevent slight from entering your eyes, put on a nap mask.

Get an top notch night time's sleep every night time.

Eat a wholesome diet plan.

There are some matters you can do if you revel in sleep paralysis.

Wiggle your fingers and ft.

Relax your mind.

Deepen your respiratory.

Think about turning. Close your eyes.

Talk to your clinical physician if you have any questions about sleep paralysis.

Ryan Hurd's e-book Sleep Paralysis - A Guide to Hypnagogic Visions, Night Visitors, it is an entire ebook almost about sleep paralysis, covers a number of those strategies.

THE POWER OF SLEEP PARALYSIS

Fear is a effective tool. Fear should make us do super topics and additionally cause us to do terrifying things. Fear can be used in the media, in advertising and in battle as a motivator, tool or weapon. Sleep paralysis is a manner of managing the most frightening memories we will hold in thoughts, for individuals who are exploring their attention. It is viable to exercising facing and accepting our fears, similarly to casting off their energy.

This fear is described within the Tibetan Book of the Dead due to the fact the mother or father of the door to the afterlife. Jung makes use of the archetypes of the shadow to provide an explanation for this worry. Traditions as severa as Christianity, Freemasonry and alchemy talk of overcoming the shadow thru confronting the concern in the archetype of demise. Although sleep paralysis can be distressing, it is critical to take the threat of lucid dreaming.

SLEEP PARALYSIS SEEN FROM ANOTHER PERSPECTIVE

It is important to just accept sleep paralysis. Accepting that the unknown is there and accepting the reality that we can't manipulate it may regularly be sufficient to cast off worry. Sleep paralysis can serve to determine if we are geared up to face fear and one-of-a-type factors of ourselves that we do now not need or need to govern.

Imagine looking a frightening film and understanding the whole film from beginning to surrender. It can be genuinely as frightening, and can even damage the a laugh. The same goes for sleep paralysis. Accepting that you're going to experience a few issue everyday, horrifying and unusual permit you to lessen the concern.

Sleep paralysis is a profound lesson for lifestyles. How typically in our lives can we react to what is going on before we can recognize it? Often that is because of worry, reluctance or worry of accepting statistics that isn't always ours or that we can't manipulate. We exercise mediating the unknown in lucid dreaming and sleep paralysis. We can be greater compassionate in our every day lives if we are able to exercise compassion for ourselves in our sleep.

You can also phrase at the same time as you dream which you are aware of your environment, it is referred to as sleep paralysis. You can use this recognition to set lucid dreaming in motion with the useful resource of truely allowing the dream to arise as you examine it. This view of sleep paralysis is one manner to free up lucid dreaming, further to to free yourself from phantom worry.

MEMORY AND REM SLEEP

A regular individual dreams about four or five times a night, and only one or goals are retained. Some goals are super a brief sound or a flash of slight. However, all are dreams. Dreams are maximum common in REM sleep. However, we also can dream at some point of NREM (or non-REM) sleep...

The tough element is not dreaming, however remembering.

In this monetary break we are capable to speak about memory and dream memory. We may additionally additionally even talk how desires can be used to beautify reminiscence.

It isn't always identified how desires are remembered. There are many theories that each offer a bit of the puzzle. When we take they all collectively, we're able to discover clues to assist us undergo in mind our goals. We can then enlarge practices to useful resource this remember.

Chapter 13: Long-Term Empowerment

Understanding how reminiscence works is important to know-how dream memory. Although this way isn't always however truly understood, one principle that has received reputation is lengthy-term potentiation (or LTP). This takes area at the same time as synapses, which might be the areas that be a part of neurotransmitters to the thoughts, keep to fireplace for a long time in a selected pattern. This activation motives a strengthening of the synapse with its neighboring synapses. This strengthens the synapse and creates a reminiscence. On the alternative hand, inactiveness can cause prolonged-time period depletion (LTD) and weaken the links that exist amongst synapses and those spherical them.

Because of the importance of LTD in prolonged-time period memories, studies on LTP has centered widely talking on the hippocampus. This is why it's far vital for dreamers. Because the hippocampus performs a vital function in goals, it converts quick-term reminiscences (the dream revel in) into lengthy-term reminiscence in different regions of the thoughts. This allows us to don't forget the dream even as we awaken. The mind releases unique neurotransmitters and hormones that allow LTD or LTP within the hippocampus. These chemical approaches are poorly understood. However, Dr. Allan Hobson of Harvard Medical School, a psychiatrist who is furthermore a dream researcher, has furnished greater notion into how dream memory works. We will communicate it underneath.

ACTIVATION-SYNTHESIS HYPOTHESIS

During REM sleep, this is the degree on the same time as we've the maximum colorful goals, there may be an growth in mind stages of the protein acetylcholine. This chemical plays a key function in strengthening synapses. Memory loss has been related to Alzheimer's patients. This is due to the fact the mechanisms that produce acetylcholine were destroyed. One possible purpose why we're capable of do not forget our goals is the increase in acetylcholine.

However, this concept has its obstacles. Each of our sleep cycles lasts approximately 90 minutes. They additionally embody the REM section. This will growth many questions. If there are various sleep phases steady with night time time time and the REM section takes place in each phase, why is it so difficult to maintain in thoughts every section? This is why it is so difficult to take into account dreams early in the night time time, or while we are not conscious after an REM section. It's not pretty a whole lot acetylcholine.

Although memory formation in desires will increase in the REM ranges of the night and morning, this suggests that dreaming is a more complicated method than sincerely imparting acetylcholine to the thoughts.

Glutamate, some other neurotransmitter under look at for its position in memory and its dating to Alzheimer's infection, is also being investigated. GABA is also suffering from glutamate, an excitatory neurotransmitter. Glutamate becomes much less active while hippocampal glutamate is active. Research has shown that materials collectively with alcohol and marijuana can bind to GABA receptors inside the hippocampus. This results in a lovely surrender quit result: the incapability to create new recollections. The memory of dreams can be restored if we allow the ones intoxicating materials disappear.

Glutamate and acetylcholine appear like the two essential culprits inside the advent of recent reminiscences. Research has additionally demonstrated that hormones are an important part of this equation.

The pineal gland hormone oxytocin.

The pineal gland is associated with goals and adjusted states of recognition. This can be as it obviously carries dimethyltryptamine in rats. The pineal gland, additionally called the 0.33 eye or the 0.33 eye, includes hormones concerned inside the sleep-wake approach, which incorporates melatonin, vasotocin and oxytocin. Although little is idea approximately the feature of oxytocin in sleep, it has a exceptional impact on memory and dreams.

When melatonin and oxytocin are released at some point of sleep, REM sleep is activated. Oxytocin is also concerned in modulating GABA and glutamate tiers inside the hippocampus. This affects the vital fearful device. The pineal gland converts serotonin to melatonin and melatonin, and melatonin hobby is highest in the morning and decreases in some unspecified time inside the destiny of the night time. The balance of this oxytocin-melatonin-serotonin cocktail may additionally make a contribution to fluctuations in our capacity to undergo in thoughts desires.

Cortisol

Cortisol is each other hassle contributing to don't forget, but it's far frequently disregarded. Cortisol, like oxytocin and melatonin, moreover follows a circadian rhythm. It is involved in reminiscence formation in the hippocampus. Cortisol ranges which is probably too high can result in hippocampal sickness. This can cause reminiscence troubles.

Cortisol, a stress hormone, can be reduced through manner of mindfulness meditation and exercising. The hippocampus can be suffering from practices which incorporates dream journaling and listening to binaural beats. Reality assessments may moreover have an effect on cortisol ranges, which may additionally provide an cause for why they appear to decorate dream don't forget.

A DREAM PILL?

Galantamine is a remedy often prescribed to Alzheimer's sufferers to provide most of the compounds needed to enhance reminiscence. Galantamine has been proven to be very powerful in improving reminiscence and lucid dreaming, in keeping with studies relationship lower back to 2006. Galantamine can assist human beings come to be greater aware of their dreams and manage them. It moreover allows lucid dreaming. Galantamine's potential to inhibit the enzyme acetylcholinesterase is what most researchers trust is the motive it's so powerful in improving recall. Acetylcholinesterase is chargeable for the breakdown of acetylcholine. Studies have shown that memory hold in mind inside the thoughts is straight away associated with acetylcholinesterase, so decreasing acetylcholinesterase may additionally help beautify memory formation. Galantamine moreover will growth mind glutamate, that is associated with reminiscence formation. This makes it a virtually powerful device for reminiscence enhancement.

Galantamine has had terrific effects on me in my view. We will communicate the viable effects and impacts of galantamine in each different financial ruin. However, it is critical that you are seeking advice from your medical doctor before taking any supplements to ensure they may be solid.

BEYOND SIMULATION

What does it advise to be aware about dreaming? Just as there are various degrees to focus, there also are many degrees to lucid dreaming. It is sort of as if you are living in a simulation. It simulates the fact which you see on the identical time as you're wakeful. You do not recognise you're in a simulation, however you enjoy it. A lucid dream is whilst you are conscious that you are in the simulation.

Just as in a video game, after you come to be familiar with the simulation you'll be able to find out the controls and perform them. Over time, you may be able to conquer the simulation and talk right away with the cause psyche if you obtain greater training and growth your cognizance.

The first diploma of lucid dreaming is without a doubt being conscious which you are dreaming. More paintings is wanted to keep past this diploma. This art work has been described in the literature on Buddhist dream yoga, Aristotle's description of being conscious in goals, spiritual paintings promoted and maintained thru the Catholic Church, further to in cutting-edge scientific studies. All of those belongings provide maps to assist us conquer the dream simulation created thru our subconscious self and input into a completely fantastic sort of dream revel in. One wherein we are able to have out-of-body memories or astral projection. It is as a first rate deal as you how a long way you go with lucid dreaming and what insights you advantage from it.

LET'S DO IT!

THE BASICS

It is usually pretty clean to have the primary sleep. Most dreamers achieve it in a matter quantity of hours in the event that they have a wholesome manner of lifestyles and a amazing bedtime normal.

There are almost as many lucid dreaming strategies as there are dreamers. This technique that, if you run into an impediment, you have many alternatives. This bankruptcy will cowl the fundamentals of lucid dreaming and provide a few strategies to assist your dreams.

Lucid dreaming can be taken into consideration a workout of recognition. Anyone can do it. You do not must be a spiritual guru to do it. But, if you do, congratulations! You simply want to take into account that you can lucid dream and then decide to exercise. By honestly immersing yourself within the thoughts of lucid dreaming, including analyzing approximately it or speakme approximately it, you can growth your possibilities of lucid dreaming.

There are severa publications that promise lucid dreaming fulfillment. There are severa guides that promise lucid dreaming success. However, few humans agree at the outstanding practices. Fewer despite the fact that are the techniques which may be first-rate for max people. Here are seven simple steps to get you commenced in your journey to lucid dreaming.

SEVEN STEPS OF THE PROCESS

Good sleep hygiene and cause placing are the principles of lucid dreaming. This is the first step to lucid dreaming. Don't rush to research extra tricks. You may be surprised how smooth actions on the facet of noticing your environment, putting sleep intentions and assisting your dream can help your mind wake up your very private potential.

These steps are a framework for lucid dreaming. These steps may be divided into three agencies: in advance than, at some stage in and after dreaming. Each institution units the level for the subsequent. It will take approximately two weeks to be aware adjustments in your capability to remember and be aware of your goals, and to enjoy lucid dreaming.

BEFORE GOING TO SLEEP

Reality take a look at: Perform truth checks within the direction of the day. Take study of the manner subjects enjoy, what meals tastes like, what your fingers seem like and the manner you've got interplay with them. This is because of the truth we often see subjects in goals that don't healthy our truth. Or which can be out of location. These errors may be the key to achieving lucidity. Ask yourself this query at a few diploma inside the day, "Am I dreaming?" If feasible, say it out loud. Next, make the effort to recall what you are questioning. Ask yourself the question after which check your waking surroundings to find out why. To help you recognize if you are dreaming, you can use reality tests to observe your waking surroundings.

Alarm: Your alarm ought to burst off four to 6 hours after waking from sleep. Your body and thoughts ought to be nicely rested before trying to lucid dream. Your REM cycles will ultimate longer the extra sleep cycles you have got. Each sleep cycle lasts about ninety minutes. Since the REM phase is related to dreaming, it's far believed that the longer the REM cycle, the greater the possibilities of having a dream or becoming lucid.

Your purpose: Say that you may have a lucid vision. You can tell yourself that your dreams may be remembered and that desires are essential.

DURING SLEEP

Get up in advance than the alarm is going off.

Relax and get ready for sleep. Get used to dreaming lucidly.

Go back to sleep: This is the hardest issue. You may be overstimulated and having hassle falling asleep. Relax and forget about approximately approximately the whole thing. You will locate that your mind will awaken obviously whilst you start this new ordinary and you'll be capable of fall again to sleep quite frequently. Your body will revel in a sleep section every hour, and then you may awaken. Try now not to move or open your eyes in the meanwhile. Although you have to be conscious which you are wide awake, try to don't forget yourself inside the lavatory replicate or visualize a face or item in your head. If viable, do now not flow. But imagine your body moving on your mind. It does no longer remember if you do now not flow, it's far adequate. You is probably capable of try many stuff before you get up and begin your day. All you have to do is loosen up and permit the enjoy spread. It will show up. If you do not forget a dream, you could interest your interest on it and take into account yourself inside the dream. Then consider what you may have completed in case you had been lucid. As if you have been lucid, don't forget the dream and make the intention to lucid dream on the identical time as you are decrease again in bed.

Chapter 14: After Dreaming

Participate: Whether you lucid dream or not, having conversations with different lucid dreamers will assist you bought the subsequent level.

REMEMBERING YOUR DREAMS

As I actually have said earlier than, remembering your dreams is the maximum critical aspect in lucid dreaming. Although we may additionally have lucid desires each night, you are not likely to keep in thoughts them. ....

Hobson, the Harvard dream researcher, claims that the hippocampus (the location of the thoughts that controls lengthy-term recollections) shuts down while we dream. Although we are able to recall factors of our goals, we frequently neglect approximately them as soon as we wake up. We might also additionally furthermore have many dreams in a single night time. Many of those dreams we do now not understand we have got had because of the truth we close to down.

There are many techniques that can be used to conquer this hassle and boom the chances of remembering dreams. These mind have been clarified and extended with the aid of me. I simply have furthermore categorised them regular with their complexity and kind. These are the fundamentals, beginning with the fundamentals and completing with superior tools for individuals who can not sleep properly sufficient to benefit lucidity. In the subsequent chapters, we are capable of take a look at some of those strategies in greater detail.

EASY

Exploring the volume and surroundings

Set and setting is a term that comes from the lexicon of psychoactive tablets. Onirologists, who take a look at dreams, have found it because of the fact the dream experience is similar to a psychedelic tour. David Jay Brown explores the connection between lucid goals and psychedelics in Dreaming Wide Awake. Set and setting is a concept that consists of listening to your surroundings and developing an surroundings that lets in you to have powerful reviews. This concept also can be carried out to lucid dreaming.

Take a go searching your mattress room to look what your surroundings looks as if. Does it sense like a place in which you could dream and sleep? Is it most effective a group of disorienting gadgets? Clear out the clutter and digital gadgets. The pineal gland, that's photosensitive, will produce melatonin if you keep the lighting fixtures off.

Configuration and adjustment additionally consist of the way you position your self in mattress. Body feature may have an effect at the splendid of lucid goals. For example, lying on your stomach might also moreover bring about extra commonplace dreams, at the same time as mendacity on your again can also produce extra out-of-frame lucid desires.

KEEPING A DREAM DIARY

A dream mag is the maximum vital tool in your lucid dreaming toolbox. Keep your lengthy-time period reminiscence energetic with dream journals. Keeping a journal can growth our functionality to endure in thoughts and preserve goals after waking up. Because it includes a mixture of mind, senses and motion, the bodily act of writing phrases and pictures in a mag also can have an impact on cognizance.

USE A SLEEP MASK

A sleep masks is crucial for dreaming if you do not sleep in complete darkness. A sleep mask no longer simplest offers the darkness wanted for great dreams, however moreover serves as a fact take a look at. If you may see actually and visit bed with the mask on, you could recognize you're dreaming.

MEDITATION AND AWARENESS

It is important to be privy to what you're doing every day to reach lucidity. Being aware about what you are doing in each second permits you to reputation on the triumphing and permits you to dream. Meditation is a super manner to clean your thoughts. Focus to your respiration and meditate. Concentrating on a selected object or in your respiratory is a terrific way to growth dream recall and decorate your possibilities of turning into lucid.

TO BE AWARE OF SLEEP PROCESSES

It is vital to understand what your body does in advance than you go to sleep. This will assist you apprehend and show screen the modifications that arise as you fall asleep. As your frame falls asleep, you can enjoy frame spasms, temperature fluctuations, seen and auditory hallucinations, in addition to unique physiological reactions. Practice searching at your specific approach. You also can set and regulate your body to result in a slightly lower frame temperature. This will motive your body's sleep cycles. You can boom your reputation through the use of mendacity to your again and running toward respiration strategies.

Using MILD

Mnemonic Induced Lucid Dreaming (MILD) is one of the extremely good techniques to bear in mind topics and increase your lucid dreaming functionality. Numerous research have tested that MILD is one of the exceptional techniques to boom your possibilities of lucid dreaming. Learn more about MILD in Chapter nine.

INTERMEDIATE

Get up and circulate!

Although it could seem counterintuitive, waking up regularly can educate your brain to replace among being awake (the us of a most associated with focus) or asleep (the state maximum related to desires). You may additionally moreover wake up extra often than you want to, that could adjust your sleep cycle and make your mind more alert even as you need to be napping. This will enhance your keep in mind of desires and your average manage over them.

Avoid alcohol

Your desires may be laid low with what you eat and drink. People revel in some beverages inside the night time. Drinking is a popular manner to loosen up and assist you sleep. There is some truth to the concept that alcohol, even in large portions, can growth the quantity of desires and recollections you have were given have been given. This is because of the fact alcohol can increase the amount of serotonin on your tool. You may additionally additionally recollect that serotonin blocks REM sleep and GABA decreases reminiscence formation. Once serotonin ranges drop, there may be a rebound from REM segment, which is an prolonged REM length than popular. GABA tiers drop and prolonged-time period reminiscence formation seems amplified.

Although REM rebound also can sound like a wonderful way to keep in thoughts lucid dream sequences, the prolonged-term horrible fitness effects of alcohol use for lucid dream induction (which consist of lack of serotonin over the years and decreased sleep first rate) are in all likelihood to outweigh the blessings.

NATURAL WAYS TO INCREASE SEROTONIN

Drinking milk earlier than bedtime or eating fish increases serotonin degrees. This can purpose REM rebound. For similar effects, you can moreover take 5-HTP earlier than bedtime. It is a natural precursor of serotonin.

MODIFY YOUR SLEEP CYCLE

It's a excellent idea to mix up your exercises in case you need to construct muscle. To have lucid dreams, you ought to additionally mix it up while you visit mattress. Your body and mind will begin to recognize even as it is regular for you to go to sleep. You can trick your mind by using changing the instances you visit mattress and awaken, a good way to make it assume you are large conscious. This will assist you become extra aware about your dreams.

TAKE INTO ACCOUNT THE SUPPLEMENTARY AID

Thomas Yuschak lists the numerous dietary supplements he attempted to decorate his lucid dreaming in his e-book Advanced Lucid Dreaming. This workout is typically known as Supplement-Induced Lucid Dreaming, which includes nutritional dietary dietary dietary supplements that lessen the amount of REM in the first half of the night time time and increase REM later within the sleep cycle. My private experiments have confirmed me that dietary dietary supplements that increase serotonin and acetylcholine production are the only for lucid dreaming.

Use warning. To make certain safety, you should are seeking for recommendation from your physician in advance than taking any supplement.

CAFFEINE

Caffeine-based totally stimulants, such as espresso and caffeine, can growth the manufacturing of different chemical substances. For this motive, many people drink these drinks to evoke. Caffeine can help human beings doze off if taken in small doses. Caffeine acts as an adenosine antagonist and might assist the conversion of serotonin into melatonin with the useful useful resource of the pineal gland. The way caffeine is consumed may be implemented in lucid dreaming (see CWILD underneath).

Caffeine-added on lucid dreaming (CWILD)

This superior technique makes use of caffeine to create an dependancy. As excessive because it sounds, this is the truth. Then the caffeine is all at once removed. Withdrawal signs and symptoms rise up and you doze off. When you are in a REM country, you're more likely to awaken. These withdrawal signs and symptoms and symptoms disappear and are a trademark that the dreamer is in a dream.

SEROTONIN

Serotonin is accountable for lowering REM section and enhancing dream undergo in mind. It is likewise cited to have sunlight hours benefits: serotonin has been tested to reduce melancholy, decorate temper and reduce the choice to overeat. Five-HTP can be used to growth serotonin production.

ACETYLCOLINE

Acetylcholine, a neurotransmitter that aids memory, is straight away related to wakefulness degrees. The frame can growth the volume of acetylcholine while slumbering through way of the use of choline salts. These salts sell the production of the neurotransmitter acetylcholine. Galantamine, an acetylcholinesterase inhibitor, may be especially powerful as it prevents the ordinary breakdown of acetylcholine and lets in it to accumulate within the brain.

HISTAMINES

Although histamines aren't frequently cited within the lucid dreaming community, they'll be crucial. Histamines are a manner of releasing serotonin in the frame. Histamines also can release a protein called PGD2, this is idea to be responsible for sleep arousal. If you are willing to be by means of using the niacin effect, niacin (or vitamins B3) is a awesome complement. Niacin can motive a skin response that releases serotonin, PGD2 and reasons a flushing of the pores and pores and skin. This is found via fatigue and a experience of rest.

CHRONOMETER

It appears that having the right nutritional nutritional supplements is half the conflict. However, it's miles in addition critical to use them efficaciously. The Wake Back to Bed (WBTB) technique is the quality (see Chapter 10).

During the day: Take a caffeinated beverage or supplement. This will result in a later withdrawal.

Daytime: Do no longer consume caffeine the day in advance than you want to have a shiny sleep.

Take a mixture of five-HTP and niacin in advance than bedtime. This will let you have extra colorful goals and also will assist you don't forget your dreams later within the night time time time after waking up.

Two hours after bedtime, wake up and complement with galantamine collectively with some caffeine. This will enhance memory and sleep cycle competence, similarly to growth REM rebound approximately four hours earlier than bedtime.

This method need to now not be used each night time, or any night time you do now not expect to get six hours of sleep.

DAILY RITUAL

It is critical to set up a each day exercising to have lucid dreams at some stage within the night time time. This manual will permit you to be everyday.

Supplements/Meditation: earlier than going to sleep, take a aggregate of niacin and 5-HTP nutritional supplements. You can relax in meditative mode the use of a respiration technique that calms you and prepares you for sleep.

When you have got completed meditating, go to sleep.

Wake up after hours of sleep. This will permit the frame to lucid dream and relaxation. Galantamine also can be taken upon awakening. Then you can wait one hour in advance than going again to sleep.

Meditation, extended REM sleep due to galantamine and a comfortable u . S . A . Make it possible as a way to have lucid goals of the WILD type.

Repeat steps C and D with out additional galantamine to strive more than one WILD goals. You can keep this tool until you are prepared to start day after today.

Write down your dreams after you awaken. This will help you reaffirm your lucid dreaming goals.

Additional meditations may be finished in the course of the day that are not associated with lucid dreaming, together with mindfulness, body attention meditations, and yoga practices. Alternate days the various lucid dreaming practices described on this ebook and the greater meditation practices.

LUCID DREAMING: THE GENTLEST FORM

Now that you have a essential examine of lucid dreaming, allow's extend at the only strategies for attaining lucidity.

The dream below suggests that I have been schooling Lucid Dreaming for a few nights every week. This come to be my first night time time time the use of the Mnemonic

Induced Lucid Dreaming (MILD) method. Although I changed into now not lucid for extraordinarily long, it have end up an awesome revel in.

I am presently taking training in university, and I am having trouble passing some of them. These goals are not unusual for me, and I am currently in university taking commands which may be out of my comfort zones. At one issue, I recognise I am dreaming and my complete body begins offevolved to go with the flow in the dream. The dream maintains, however I speedy lose consciousness.

This experience taught me that MILD can be a powerful device if used correctly. Stephen LaBerge's peer-reviewed research positioned that MILD can not simplest bring about lucid dreaming, but additionally notably improve the dreamers' capability to lucid dream.

Mnemonics are a common reminiscence method that you could have placed out in university. It works because of the reality our brains find out it a whole lot less hard to bear in thoughts records that has been visualized than to retrieve data this is greater complex and difficult to visualise. That's why acronyms are less difficult to consider than prolonged phrases. These identical techniques can be used in lucid dreaming. I talk over with them as reminiscence bridges, which can be reference points that hyperlink the events of a dream to a acquainted feeling, sound or occasion. These feelings, sounds and activities can resultseasily become seen reminiscences.

LaBerge had studies contributors awaken inside the midnight to endure in mind their goals and then agree with what have to have occurred in the event that they were lucid. Participants could attention on this idea after which pass decrease again to bed with the reason of getting a lucid night time time. They may additionally take into account their beyond goals as even though they had been lucid. This reminiscence gadget allowed the dreamers to be lucid within the subsequent dream thru growing the mnemonic sample that our thoughts craves.

HOW TO DO IT

Here is a short precis of the MILD technique.

You can doze off with the reason of getting a lucid dream.

Stand up and stay your dream.

As when you have been having lucid dreams, don't forget the dream you honestly had. Imagine what you will do if it have been a lucid dream.

You can skip decrease again to sleep and consider your preceding dream as if you have been having a dream.

For MILD, the maximum important issue is to remember your previous dream as in case you had been lucid. Many human beings talk about repeating the concept that you may have lucid goals over and over once more earlier than going to bed. However, this is not the excellent approach as it does not stimulate the thoughts in the identical manner as the MILD technique. It is possible to create a connection with the dream you in reality had and accept as true with it as lucid. This will permit our mind to endure in mind that lucid goals are feasible. We educate ourselves thru asking "If you could lucid dream, what would it not not were like?".

It is simple to appearance how MILD works. After having a dream that modified into not lucid, the brain creates a intellectual photograph of itself having a lucid dream. This places the thoughts in a innovative country and lets in you to experience the enjoy. Imagine that you have had a lucid dream. This brings lucid dreaming closer and allows our brain to see it as feasible. We can allow our mind to lucid dream through growing the reminiscence-creativeness connection.

www.ingramcontent.com/pod-product-compliance
Lightning Source LLC
Chambersburg PA
CBHW071444080526
44587CB00014B/1979